GW00632320

WHO RUNS THE WORLD?

**Written for Christian Aid
by John Madeley, Dee Sullivan
and Jessica Woodroffe**

Published in 1994 by Christian Aid
PO Box 100, London SE1 7RT

Page make-up by Devious Designs

Cover photograph: Christian Aid/Salomon Cytrynowicz

Cartoons by Polyp

Printed in the UK by Blackmore Press, Shaftesbury

ISBN: 0 904379 20 5

Copyright © Christian Aid 1994

Contents

Preface

If you ask people, as we did, 'Who runs the world?', you get a variety of answers. Some name individuals, like the Queen or the President of the USA or the owners of tabloid newspapers. Others point to to large, faceless institutions like banks, multinationals or 'the Establishment' in general. But people are agreed on one thing. Running the world is all about the control of money. Power in our world is essentially seen as *economic* power.

Boring old economics

Curiously, they also agreed that reading or thinking about economics is boring. Somehow we find ourselves in a society which reckons that its most important source of power – the control of money – is too difficult for most people to think about. Economics is a specialist field that you have to be an expert to understand. It's all right to skip over the financial pages of the newspaper because in any case we don't *have* to think about those things.

Many Christians seem to share this lack of interest. Few connections are made between economic issues and matters of faith – except perhaps the obligation to give to charity. Faith is widely regarded as personal and spiritual only, while economics belongs in the realm of politics. So when church leaders make remarks about poverty and wealth, they are criticised for stepping out of line. Christians differ on economic matters, so churches should stay neutral.

Experts at the sharp end

But growing numbers of people in the Third World don't have the luxury of thinking that economic theories are boring or neutral. They are becoming experts at the sharp end, where the economic policies of the **World Bank** and the **International Monetary Fund** are having a daily and devastating impact on their lives. As this book graphically shows, families as far apart as Zimbabwe, Bolivia and Sri Lanka, who used to be able to manage their own lives and feed their children, are finding that now they can't. For them, large-scale economic policies, which are supposed to lead their countries into economic health, translate into immediate and urgent questions. Can they afford medicine any more? Or schooling for their children? Will there be bread on the table? Does the market price for their crops make it worth the effort of harvesting them at all? Will it ever be possible to earn a living wage? Above all, when there is competition between people who are all grindingly poor, what happens to any sense of community? Why are these things happening, and who is running the world this way?

Economics and the Bible

So economic policies are neither boring nor morally neutral. They have a human impact which is crying out to be addressed. And the Bible has always known this. Its teaching about wealth and poverty is extensive – a great many parables, laws, prophetic sermons and dire warnings (both general and specific) are found to deal with economic matters. It seems that God is *very interested in economics*. And that's just the Old

Filipino fishermen catch fish using technology called Paragdig – a net is suspended from two bamboo piers in the sea. Fishermen search under the net for fish, lighting paraffin lamps at night to attract them.

CHRISTIAN AID/STUART FRANKLIN

Testament. Jesus is known to have made several uncomfortable remarks about wealth. In the same vein, early Christian writers agonised about whether or not the rich people in their communities could be saved at all. Economic activity and its relation to the gospel message was of primary importance then, and continued to be a recurring preoccupation throughout many centuries of Christianity. Whole religious movements like the Franciscans sprang up to address the question. The tradition of moral neutrality towards the use of money is actually an odd modern phenomenon. So perhaps Christians should get back to their roots on the subject.

Biblical roots and big money

What then are our biblical resources for examining the workings of those institutions that handle big money?

- The Bible doesn't let us get away with believing that morality only applies to individuals. Old Testament laws always apply to the moral sickness or health of a whole society. And the gospel call to the Kingdom of God is about a transformed community on earth.

So we can't say that political or economic matters don't concern Christians.

- Biblical laws about economic matters (such as debt, trade, and ownership of land) start from the impact of business practice on the poorest and most vulnerable. Behaviour that destroys the poor person without mercy is always condemned.

So if our financial institutions destroy poor people they must be judged.

- One of the recurring concerns of the Bible is the seduction of 'other gods': idols, Mammon, etc. The main reason for failing to worship the true God is our unchallenged and sinful allegiance to other sources of power in our world.

So if we accept powerful financial systems without question we may fall into sin.

- The Bible constantly offers visions, articulated by those who are poor or persecuted by present reality, about how things could be different.

So we are called to dream about God's will done on earth.

More detailed exposition of these themes is found in the booklet ***Who Runs the World?*** – *ideas for worship leaders,* available free from Christian Aid.

Who runs the world?

This is why Christian Aid, along with other organisations like UNICEF is asking its supporters to be involved in a campaign to assess the work and present impact of the **World Bank** and the **International Monetary Fund.** Their current policies are intended to help poor nations move out of poverty and into economic health. But our stance is:

* Their policies are not working for the poor but effectively destroying the lives of many, and we must expose this.
* Their power to dictate to the economies of poor nations is too great, and we must hold them accountable.
* Alternative strategies could be tried, and poor people themselves should have the right to shape their future.

Making a difference

It is easy to feel helpless when faced with trying to change things that are so big and apparently well out of our control. But we are not alone and there is action that we can take. People whose work Christian Aid supports in the South are asking us urgently to do what we can to influence the policies of these institutions, which are funded and run by wealthier Northern countries. Along with other agencies, Christian Aid supporters have been able to make a real difference through a concerted effort to understand the big global factors that keep people poor, and to bring pressure to bear. We have together helped shape public opinion and actual banking and trading policies through our work on the Third World debt and on unfair trading practice. This campaign takes one step further into trying to reach the roots of poverty, and this book gives the stories, the facts and the analysis to help us do that. It will not be easy, but neither will it be boring.

CHAPTER I

Who runs the world?

Betty Mozira watched as her three-year-old grandson played with a stick in the dusty ground. An ex-teacher and twice widowed, Betty lives with two grandchildren in a village near Bulawayo in Zimbabwe. Since retiring as a matron in 1984, she has made ends meet by selling knitted clothes and rag rugs and mending clothes for her neighbours. But now she is finding it much harder to get by.

"I used to sew and go to Matebele and even further to sell my things, but now, because people are not working, they cannot afford to buy," Betty explains in her strong, throaty voice. "Also, I cannot afford the bus fare when I hardly have enough money to buy food for myself and two grandchildren. Now I sell only a few things to people here in the villages.

Betty Mozira (centre) hangs up slices of melon to dry.

CHRISTIAN AID/GIDEON MENDEL

"In this area, people who had cattle now don't. Even when the cattle survived the drought, people sold their cows, donkeys and goats to buy food and clothes. Then in January prices rocketed and things got even worse. Now bread and maize are very expensive. We used to eat them all the time; now families have to eat less."

Not only in Zimbabwe but throughout the Third World, poor families are being hit hard. Their story is simple and tragic: the most vulnerable people are bearing the heaviest burden. People are being thrown out of work and are unable to eat properly; children are cut off from the education that is vital for their future; millions are no longer able to afford basic health care services. Why has this happened?

A deadly exchange

Betty Mozira makes no bones about it. It is, she says, because the Zimbabwe government drastically changed the economy, by introducing policies which Zimbabweans call ESAP. "And ESAP is killing us," she says firmly. People throughout the Third World are battling to survive in the face of policies like Zimbabwe's ESAP, which are known collectively as Structural Adjustment Programmes (SAPs). Governments of Third World countries introduce SAPs in exchange for aid and loans from the World Bank and the IMF. These policies are supposed to lead to economic growth, but in most countries they have failed to do even this. And even when growth has occurred, the poor have often been left out – millions of people are now poorer than when these policies began. SAPs, imposed by distant financial institutions like the World Bank and the IMF, have had a devastating effect on the lives of ordinary people, like Betty Mozira.

A world apart

To people in Third World countries it seems that the World Bank and the IMF now run the world. Certainly their world. "The Caribbean doesn't belong to the Caribbean people, it belongs to the IMF and the World Bank", says Margaret Pierre of the Caribbean Conference of Churches, one of Christian Aid's partners.

Why, then, do Third World countries get involved with the World Bank and the IMF?

A world off balance: debt and unfair trade

Even before SAPs came on the scene, Third World countries were already in great difficulties. In some, a few people with influence in government or business had sufficient power to protect or even enrich themselves, while neglecting the interests of the majority of the people. And on top of that, the people of the Third World were already suffering because of the debt crisis and the unfair international trading system. So SAPs made a bad situation even worse.

The debt crisis

The debt crisis hit Third World countries in the early 1980s. Governments had borrowed money from commercial banks in the 1970s when interest rates were low, to cover the cost of rocketing oil prices and to build and improve necessities such as roads, schools and factories. Then world interest rates suddenly soared as a result of European and American economic policies. At the same time, the price of goods exported by many Third World countries, like coffee, tea and sugar, slumped dramatically. Governments found that the amount of money they could earn from exports fell sharply.

Both factors were beyond the control of the Third World and left governments unable to repay their debts. Many countries were faced with an awful choice: should they use the little money they had to repay their debts, to improve their agricultural production, or to heal their sick? President Julius Nyerere of Tanzania was forced to ask, "Must we starve our children to pay our debts?"

Unfair trade

The Third World's burden of debt was not, however, the whole story. It was equally clear that countries were not getting a fair deal from the international trading system. As the prices of export goods such as cocoa and coffee fell, the farmers who grew them became ever more unable to make ends meet. And the rich countries of the North put up trade barriers to protect their own industries and agriculture, denying many Third World countries markets for their goods.

Debt repayments and an inability to earn money from trade meant that Third World countries desperately needed money. Yet commercial banks were no longer willing to lend, now that

they sensed their loans might not be repaid. So countries had to turn to international organisations like the IMF and the World Bank.

A tale of two powers

The World Bank and the IMF are two of the most powerful organisations in the world, yet many people in the UK may not know who they are or what they do. But the impact of World Bank and IMF policies on ordinary people's lives is so strong that in Zimbabwe, Bolivia and many other countries across the Third World today, there is an astonishing level of knowledge and discussion about both.

The listening bank?

The World Bank is not an international version of a high street bank, operating simply to make a profit. Its function is to lend money to poorer countries to help them restore economic growth and to alleviate poverty. In 1992 Lewis Preston, president of the World Bank, said: "Sustainable poverty reduction is the overarching objective of the World Bank. It is the bench mark by which our performance as a development institution will be measured."

The World Bank is in fact the world's largest development agency. It receives a great deal of money from the aid budgets of richer countries like Britain and Ireland. But even though taxpayers' money makes up aid budgets, British and Irish taxpayers have little say in how their money is spent, and the activities of the World Bank and IMF are seldom discussed in the British and Irish parliaments.

SAPs: no such thing as free aid

The aid and loans that the World Bank and the IMF both offer to Third World countries are not simply handed out. There are strings attached – in particular, SAPs. And it is these conditions that are the problem.

Two of the aims of SAPs are to enable countries to repay their debts and, eventually, to increase economic growth. SAPs usually require countries to cut their public (or government) spending, reduce the role of government (privatising industry, removing controls on minimum wages, etc) and increase exports.

"You can't eat stability"

But this process has its hidden costs, which usually hit the poor hardest of all: job losses, cuts in health and education, and price rises. SAPs do promise 'jam tomorrow', but it's a concept scorned by Betty Mozira's friend Miriam. "That will be 15 years or more. We have to suffer now. We have to be hungry." The problem is that millions have no bread today.

"You can't eat stability," says Celia Ticono do Median, as she crouches at the dirt road in a Bolivian town with a huge pile of potatoes spread in front of her. She does not think very much of her country's SAP, designed to bring 'stability' to Bolivia's economy. Her husband lost his job as a result of it. Having journeyed all night carrying the potatoes, Celia will sit there as long as it takes to make a few dollars.

Nor does Mercedes think much of structural adjustment. Mercedes lives in Butuan, a town in the southern Philippines. Her husband lost his job when the local timber yards closed. Mercedes tried to earn a living for the family by selling home-made rice cakes at the local bus station. But IMF policies forced up the price of basic foods, among them rice; and, in an effort to generate more income, the government levied new taxes on fuel, including the kerosene with which Mercedes cooked her rice cakes. Mercedes and her street-trader friends then started to borrow money from a local money lender who charged them interest of one peso a day on every four pesos borrowed – a staggering rate of 9,125 per cent a year.

Third World governments are now implementing policies which hurt the poor – but why? The simple answer is that most of these countries were over a barrel. They needed money; to get the money they had to accept the strings attached. Other governments actively welcomed SAPs, and agreed with the policies proposed.

Change certainly had to happen if Third World countries were to meet the needs of their peoples, and escape the debt trap. But it needed to happen in a sensitive way, at a pace and in a form designed to accommodate everyone's needs. A serious charge against the World Bank and the IMF is that, through their structural adjustment policies, they concentrated only on the *domestic* changes they felt were needed. The two organisations ignored the international factors, such as unfair trade, that were keeping people poor.

CHRISTIAN AID/SALOMON CYTRYNOWICZ

Julia Escobar, vegetable seller in the market at Cochabamba, Bolivia.

Christian Aid's campaign

The crisis in the Third World is bringing millions of people to their knees. But why should Christian Aid and its supporters get involved with a problem which is, after all, in the hands of the international financial institutions? What on earth can they do about it?

Christian Aid believes that there are options for change, and that anyone concerned about justice will want to act. We believe our supporters will want to take action when they learn that they already contribute towards the problem – through their taxes. British and Irish taxpayers automatically contribute around £10 a year to the World Bank, yet there is almost no debate about how their money is used, even if it is used in ways which harm the world's poor.

The heart of our work

Helping people like Betty, Celia and Mercedes by tackling what causes their poverty lies at the heart of Christian Aid's work. It is clear that their lives are being made worse by SAPs. And these policies are impeding the development work carried out by Christian Aid's partner organisations – so it is our responsibility to act, and to do so quickly.

We know there are alternatives. World Bank and IMF policies impose a style of development which is essentially non-democratic. People are not consulted over these policies, even though they affect fundamental aspects of their lives; and this is one of the key reasons why there is so much protest against them. Although they appear to have become more aware of the negative social effects of SAPs, the World Bank and the IMF continue with them. Yet there are different approaches to development which put people at the heart of policy. In Sindebele, one of the languages spoken in Zimbabwe, the word for 'development' means taking control over what you need to work with. The World Bank, the IMF and every aid donor could learn from the philosophy behind this definition.

A continuing campaign

Many countries needed some economic changes, but Christian Aid disagrees with the single economic view of the World Bank and the IMF, which is based on policies that were only

ROMULO REGALADO

Making rice dumplings for sale to construction workers in the Philippines.

partially successful in the developed world in the 1980s. **Trade for Change,** Christian Aid's campaign for people-friendly trade, focused on goods which give more back to the producers. **Who Runs the World?,** Christian Aid's new campaign on the World Bank and the IMF, is about people-friendly development – economic growth which improves the quality of people's lives, not just a country's balance sheets.

Seizing the day – for change

In 1994 the World Bank and the IMF will be 50 years old. Their birthdays – celebrated between 1994 and 1996 – offer a unique opportunity for Christian Aid and others to speak out about the basic principles that should guide them. A wide cross-section of churches, non-governmental organisations and UN aid agencies do not believe that the World Bank and the IMF are tackling poverty effectively. They believe there are alternatives to SAPs, and they are joining together to campaign for changes in the way the World Bank and IMF work. They are concentrating more of their efforts on the World Bank, partly because development is more clearly part of its mandate, and partly because, to its credit, the World Bank is more accessible than the IMF.

CHAPTER 2

The World Bank and IMF revealed

"The health, the growth, the education and life of millions of children will be sacrificed on the altar of... economic adjustment programmes".

(UNICEF, 1990)

Beginnings: a hotel in New Hampshire

In 1944, some 700 delegates from all over the world met for three weeks at the Mount Washington Hotel in Bretton Woods, New Hampshire, USA, to discuss how to put the world back on its feet after the Second World War. The resulting articles of agreement signed on July 22 that year set up the World Bank and the IMF. The Brazilian delegate, in his final speech, said that the organisations were "inspired by a single ideal – that happiness be distributed throughout the face of the earth".

At the time, the IMF's role was seen as ensuring that countries kept to an orderly system of trade, paying each other for the goods they purchased. If a country had problems paying for its imports, it could borrow from a central fund of foreign exchange held by the IMF.

The World Bank was to support economic development by providing loans for practical development projects, such as building roads or power plants. It was supposed to lend money to Eastern Europe, but that region was soon receiving substantial funding from the USA's own aid programme for Europe, the Marshall Plan. So the World Bank switched to lending to Third World projects instead.

A third important international organisation was set up in the aftermath of Bretton Woods. The General Agreement on Tariffs and Trade (GATT) was to complement the IMF's role by negotiating rules and standards for conducting international trade and by removing barriers to trade. Yet in practice, both the IMF and the GATT favour stronger, wealthy nations over the poorer ones they were intended to help.

How the World Bank and the IMF operate

The World Bank makes loans which, until 1960, were always paid back with interest. However, during the 1950s the Bank was criticised for not responding adequately to the needs of the poorest nations, who were unable to afford the interest rates charged on normal loans. So from 1960 the World Bank started making loans, through the International Development Association, to the poorest countries at little interest, with repayment periods of up to 50 years. These 'soft' loans are financed from the aid budgets of governments like the UK and Ireland – and so ultimately, from our taxes.

Financial help from the World Bank takes two forms: projects, and programme aid (SAPs).

World Bank projects

There are many kinds of Bank-funded projects, and some do benefit the poor. But over the whole range, the success rate has been falling. In 1993 the World Bank published a review of its performance, known as the Wapenhans Report. It showed that, according to its own criteria, 37.5 per cent of projects were unsatisfactory in 1992 compared with 15 per cent in 1981. The criteria adopted by the World Bank are yet more worrying: in this key report, the Bank defines a project's success not by whether it reduces poverty, but by whether it is economically viable.

World Bank-funded projects which displace people have caused special difficulty. The most infamous is that of the Narmada dam in India, where thousands of people have been forced to leave their homes and watch their land flooded to create a dam to provide electricity, not for themselves but for other cities. There have been numerous cases of human rights abuses against those who have tried to protest. Eventually the campaign of the people of Narmada forced the Bank to withdraw its loans; but the damage has been done, and the flooding has already started.

Rio Branco

Rio Branco is a tiny hamlet just two hours outside the city of São Paulo in Brazil. There, 200 Guarani Indians are in danger of losing their livelihoods and culture because of three dams to be built at a cost of £140 million, £80 million of which is from the World Bank.

The Guarani are hunter-gatherers and need large amounts of land to sustain them. They fear that if the dam project goes ahead, the Rio Branco river they depend on for fishing and for water will dry up. This would cause untold damage to the Guarani and their environment.

The dams are meant to help São Paulo's poor, a population now growing at the astronomical rate of 200,000 a year. But, although water is desperately needed in the shantytowns, dams are not the solution. Instead, the polluted Billings Reservoir and the River Tiete could be cleaned up and used to supply water – a project the Water Board plans to put into effect no earlier than 2005.

In April 1994, World Bank staff were clear that they had consulted organisations in the region and as a result had closed down a small part of the project. In their opinion the remaining dams would not impact on the Guarani.

But Christian Aid partner organisation, the Indigenous Missionary Council (CIMI), were adamant that no World Bank staff had visited the Guarani village of Rio Branco or consulted with the Guarani who live there. In May 1994, Darci Jose Ciconetti of CIMI and representatives of the Rio Branco Community, stated, "We have never agreed to this project as it will seriously affect us and cause us unforeseeable consequences".

Tupamao Guarani plays guitar. The Guarani Indians are threatened by a World Bank attempt to use the local river for dam building.

21

The dam projects at Narmada and Rio Branco (see box) are only two examples of problems with projects involving resettlement. A report prepared by the World Bank in 1993 listed many other examples where people have been left homeless after resettlement. The resettlement report concluded that, in India, "the overall record is poor to the extent of being unacceptable".

The rise of SAPs

Both the World Bank and the IMF fund programme aid, known as SAPs. By the end of the 1980s, many Third World countries had accepted SAPs as a way of getting themselves out of their terrible difficulties with debt and disappearing trade.

Between 1982 and 1987 the total foreign debt of developing countries almost doubled, rising from $650 billion to $1,190 billion. High rates of interest on the world market turned this debt into an intolerable burden and diverted resources that the Third World urgently needed for development into the industrialised countries.

So the World Bank and IMF stepped in. As we have seen, the IMF helps countries with their debt repayments if they agree to strict conditions on economic policy to become creditworthy again. Increasingly the World Bank also lent money in exchange for structural reform of the economy rather than just individual projects. About six per cent of World Bank loans were of this type in 1981; by the early 1990s, the figure was 25 per cent.

The package of reform conditions attached to World Bank and IMF loans became known as SAPs. Between 1980 and 1992, over 70 countries had received loans for SAPs, totalling $43 billion.

The World Bank's 1982 Annual Report explains why it embarked on SAPs. SAPs are "designed to achieve a more efficient use of resources, and contribute to a more sustainable balance of payments... and to the maintenance of growth".

Sceptics argue that in fact the World Bank was anxious to lend more money so that it could have more influence over the policies adopted by Third World governments. In particular, SAPs appeared to be designed to ensure that debt repayments were made and a sufficient supply of cheap raw materials was ensured – two factors which helped the rich countries in the North more than they helped the Third World.

World-wide influence

It is vital that the World Bank and IMF get their policies right because they are so influential. Over the decade 1982/3 to 1991/92, the average proportion of Britain's aid budget contribution to the World Bank Group and IMF was roughly 13 per cent. The total contribution for 1993/94 was about £239 million, 10.5 per cent of Britain's aid budget. The Irish government, in 1993, gave just over eight per cent of its total aid spending to the World Bank and the IMF.

Much of the UK bilateral aid, and debt relief, are conditional on SAPs. Most firms which are considering investing in a Third World country will also want to ensure that the government has been given the 'IMF seal of approval'. If a government wants to follow its own path rather than that of the IMF and World Bank, it stands to lose loans and business from all sources, not just the IMF or World Bank loan.

What is a SAP?

Theoretically, a SAP is an economic package agreed after negotiations between the World Bank, the IMF and the

government that needs to borrow money. But it is a negotiation between very unequal parties, as the Third World government has little to offer and nowhere else to turn. And the similar nature of SAPs across continents reinforces the view that SAPs are actually designed by the World Bank and IMF, not the borrower government.

Key issues which SAPs take into account include balance of payment deficits, inflation, the role of government, and trade.

Balance of payments

One immediate aim of a SAP is to ensure that a country does not buy more from abroad than it can pay for, and that it earns enough to pay its debts. So more export goods are sold abroad, fewer foreign import goods are purchased, and the currency is devalued, making the country's exports cheaper and more able to compete abroad.

Inflation

Inflation – an increase in prices, coupled with a fall in money's purchasing power – is seen as a significant problem. It is tackled by keeping interest rates high and restricting the amount of credit that is available. People are encouraged to spend less and save more.

Role of government

SAPs stipulate that governments bring their spending in line with their income (usually from taxes). Governments are also told to reduce their role in the economy "to promote economic efficiency by freeing the market of government controls". In practice, this means privatisation and the removal of subsidies and price controls.

Increased trade

Third World countries are encouraged to trade more on the international market. Exports are promoted, particularly traditional commodities such as coffee, sugar and cocoa. Barriers to importing foreign goods are removed. Foreign companies are encouraged to invest, often by offering them incentives, such as tax breaks.

Effect of SAPS

The standard SAP package includes the following:

GOAL	HOPED FOR EFFECTS	COMMON EFFECTS
Free-up the market (reduce government intervention):		
• reduce import controls	Competition from cheap imports forces producers to become efficient.	Competition from cheap imports puts local factories and farms out of work. (People lose their jobs and leave home to look for other work.)
• reduce government subsidies and price controls	Only efficient producers survive. Government spending reduced.	Prices of basic goods rise. Prices of farm inputs like fertilisers rise. People are worse off, and can afford less food, schooling, health etc.
• privatise	Inefficient government-run systems are closed down. Opportunities for corruption reduced.	Remote and poor areas lose essential services, because it is not profitable for the private sector to provide them.
Devalue the currency	Exports are cheaper to foreign buyers so more are sold.	Land is used for cash crops rather than food. Many countries try to sell the same goods so the price falls.
	Imports become more expensive so fewer are bought.	Increase price of imports like medicines and vital equipment for industry and farming.
Tackle inflation and reduce government deficit:		
• very high interest rates	Control money supply. People will reduce their spending.	Companies and farmers can't afford to borrow, and so reduce production or go out of business.
• reduce government spending	Reduce budget deficit.	Government services to the rural poor often easiest to cut.
Safety nets, eg food for work or income support for poorest	Protect the poorest whilst SAP restarts the economy.	Many people left out. The economy often does not restart. Lack of funds to resource.

The impact of SAPs: unsafe practice

After a storm of protest in the 1980s, modern SAPs were equipped with safety nets supposedly to protect the worst-hit people. But they are not working because governments do not have enough money to fund them. So ordinary people are left battling for survival while the basic services on which they rely are being put beyond their reach.

Throughout the Third World, the message is clear: SAPs spell hardship for people in every aspect of their lives – health, education, work, culture. The next section shows how, by examining six countries: Bolivia, Zimbabwe, Sri Lanka, Jamaica, Senegal and the Philippines.

Health: sick services

Ironically, SAPs increase the need for health care among the poorest, while actually decreasing the likelihood of their receiving it. How does this happen? Lower incomes and higher prices caused by SAPs often mean less food for the people and so more malnutrition among them. Also, families have less time to spend on health-related activities, such as food preparation and fetching clean water, because they have to work longer hours just to make ends meet.

At the same time, cuts in government spending, dictated by SAPs, have usually meant cuts in health provision. Some people on very low incomes are now expected to pay for health services that were previously free, and many services are being cut altogether. The Director-General of the World Health Organization directly blames SAPs for the recent cholera epidemic in Latin America.

There is no shortage of statistics to illustrate this point. The number of women dying in childbirth in Harare, Zimbabwe, for example, more than doubled in the first two years after that country had adopted ESAP – from 101 in 1989 to 242 in 1991. Diseases such as cholera and tuberculosis, which had been virtually eradicated in Zimbabwe, have begun to reappear; in 1992, 109 people died in a cholera outbreak. Zimbabwean government health spending fell by one-third in the first three years of ESAP, to the lowest level since independence in 1980. There is a similar story in Jamaica. In the mid 1970s, over nine per cent of the Jamaican government's budget was spent on health. By 1988 – 11 years after the introduction of Jamaica's

Going to school in Zimbabwe.

SAP – this had fallen to just over five per cent. Over the past 15 years, public service health provision in both rural and urban areas has declined substantially. There is a shortage of medicines, equipment and medical staff and the number of doctors per person in the public sector has been almost halved. "People give birth to their babies unattended", says Horace Levy from Jamaica's Social Action Centre.

Education: impossible choices

To reduce government spending, charges for education have been introduced under some SAPs. This puts parents on low incomes in a position no parent would ever want to face – either having to pay up, or take their children out of school. In Zimbabwe in 1992, secondary school enrolment fell by half in some schools. Yet only two years earlier, Zimbabwe had almost achieved its goal of secondary school education for all.

The 1994 World Bank report, *Adjustment in Africa*, admits that putting resources into primary education is "the key to achieving rapid growth in the best performing Asian economies". Yet SAPs usually have the reverse effect. Zimbabwe increased its education and health spending by over 30 per cent in the 1980s. But in the three years since 1990

27

when ESAP began, primary school spending per child has dropped from Z$400 to Z$220; secondary school spending from Z$600 to Z$440; and health spending per person from Z$50 to Z$30.

"ESAP is a monster," declared elderly Mr Gumede in Zimbabwe, talking about how children are being deprived of education. "The children are being cut off from their future. I can't imagine an illiterate person in the next century, they will have no place. In the long run it is our children's futures which are being undermined."

Girls usually suffer the most. Boys are often seen as more likely to get jobs; and training for a life outside the family is seen as a natural preparation for their future roles and responsibilities. So when faced with the choice as to which child the family can afford to send to school, it is very often the girls who are withdrawn.

Work: a crumbling support

SAPs almost always lead to unemployment. Since the introduction of structural adjustment in Bolivia in 1985, 35,000 jobs have been lost in factories simply because trade barriers were removed, which allowed competition from cheap imports. Workers are given redundancy letters which state that the reason for being made unemployed is due to the need to rationalise the workforce, as specified by the SAP. The number of people out of work rose from 15.5 per cent to 21.5 per cent between 1986 and 1989.

At the same time, working conditions in Bolivia have deteriorated. Employers can hire and fire at will. There is no minimum wage and no unemployment benefit. Sixty per cent of Bolivians in urban areas now work in the informal sector (as street sellers, for example); and this figure includes an increasing number of children who leave school to support their families.

Women have not traditionally had the same access as men to jobs in the formal sector. Consequently they have shown greater flexibility and resilience in opportunities in the informal sector, such as street selling. However, the flood of like-minded people onto an already saturated market has made survival more difficult for these women.

Caballero Robledo worked in a construction company in Cochabamba until 1985, when his wage was frozen and food prices kept going up. His wife was facing increasing

competition selling bread in the market and they could no longer make ends meet. "Now we buy and sell coca [used for cocaine] for a living, transporting the sacks to the warehouse in Cochabamba in a truck, bus or van".

Export processing zones: cheapened labour

SAPs often encourage the setting up of export processing zones (EPZs), also known as free trade zones. EPZs are normally situated on an industrial estate near a seaport or airport. The estate will house companies, usually foreign-owned, that have been attracted there by inducements such as cheap factories, cheap labour and low taxes.

Third World governments have allocated substantial amounts of scarce funds to attract companies into these zones. While the extra jobs created have been welcome, there is often a high price to pay. EPZs employ mainly unskilled and semi-skilled workers, and any skills acquired on the job are often unusable outside the plant. Wages are usually rock-bottom and working conditions poor: incentives offered to foreign companies sometimes suspend labour laws. In the Philippines, for example, foreign companies are employing a constant turnover of workers for only five months because, after six months, they would be entitled to employment protection and benefits. The quality of jobs in EPZs is crucial if the poor are really to benefit.

Small businesses: failed enterprises

SAPs have encouraged people to become entrepreneurs but have not subsequently provided them with the support they need or with markets for their products. This, together with high interest rates and costs, has meant that many small businesses have collapsed.

Margarita Llampa was a peasant farmer in Bolivia. When she could no longer support herself from her land, she was forced to turn to tailoring to make a living. She and her family now run a small workshop, producing up to eight dozen pairs of jeans a week. One dozen pairs can sell for US$55 but material alone costs US$36. The profit is eaten up by washing and transport costs – taking the jeans on a nine-hour bus journey to the capital, La Paz, to sell – and by food costs, household bills and keeping five children in school. Margarita wants a loan to buy bigger, more cost-effective machinery, but the banks will not give the association of which she is a member a loan. "It's getting more and more difficult all the time," she says. "The market is totally saturated, there is nowhere to sell."

Margarita Llampa with finished clothes at the tailoring workshop.

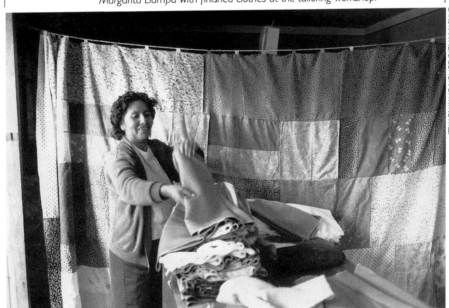

CHRISTIAN AID/SALOMON CYTRYNOWICZ

Food and farmers

Under SAPs the rural poor are supposed to benefit from increases in crop prices. However, many poor farmers do not have the resources to increase their production or to switch easily to more profitable crops. It is the large agro-businesses who really benefit.

In Jamaica, farmers cannot afford to borrow the money they need to increase their production. Those people who do have money prefer to put it in the bank, rather than risk lending it to a small agriculture or manufacturing business. Commercial interest rates are well over 20 per cent, but in any case, farmers cannot borrow money unless they can offer something as security against a loan, which is impossible for most.

Farmers in Jamaica also face high prices for imports like fertilisers, seeds and equipment, because of the devaluation of the Jamaica dollar. Restrictions on imported food have been removed, so imported onions are now on the shelves while local onion producers cannot earn enough even to cover their costs.

In an attempt to reduce its spending, the Filipino government has almost halved its budget for agriculture over the last decade. Peasant farmers' credit, post-harvest facilities and marketing support have all been cut. The government-funded rice marketing board, which buys rice at a guaranteed price, is being phased out and farmers will be left to sell their rice on the market, which is controlled by a just a few companies. Peasant farmers cannot compete with the cheap imports of rice coming in from Thailand. Under the 'Philippines 2000' programme, which aims to industrialise the country by the turn of the century, large landowners are encouraged to sell their land for factories or tourism, leaving peasant farmers without their means of survival.

Export crops

SAPs can have a dangerous effect on a country's ability to feed itself. Farmers who grow cash crops for export usually receive higher prices, and the support for small farmers is often reduced. This means that more crops and dairy produce are exported and less food is grown – a policy which has taken hold in some of the most famine-prone countries. Often, too, the export crop brings income for men, whereas the previous food crop was handled by women.

Despite the fact that Zimbabwe is a drought-prone country,

grain reserves were sold off under ESAP, and in 1992, during the worst drought for 50 years, Zimbabwe exported maize while its people were going hungry. The effects of the 1992 drought were therefore much harsher than they should have been, as Bernard Chidzero, Senior Minister of Finance, admitted to Christian Aid. "Not enough was given to the contingency for drought – agreed... We underestimated, we didn't reckon on a severe drought. The lesson we have learnt is that food security is of the highest importance."

Migration to towns and cities

A good measure of increased poverty in rural areas is the number of people who migrate to urban areas, looking for work when they can no longer make ends meet from their land.

The population of Cochabamba in Bolivia soared from 292,700 in 1983 to 580,000 in 1993, an annual growth rate of over ten per cent. Many of the people flooding into the city were ex-miners, put out of their jobs when mines closed as a result of the SAP and the collapse of tin prices.

In the Philippines, migration is not just about moving from

Living on the streets in Harare, Zimbabwe.

CHRISTIAN AID/GIDEON MENDEL

village to city. The Freedom from Debt Coalition, an organisation supported by Christian Aid, has described how women have become one of the Philippines' most lucrative exports under structural adjustment. Large numbers of Filipina women are forced to look for work in Japan, the Middle East and Europe, so that their families back home have enough money to live on.

Homelessness: on the streets

In many countries, migration to cities has led to a rise in homelessness. The bus stop area by the main railway station in Harare is where some 50 to 60 Zimbabweans sleep rough every night under thin blankets, hessian sacking or cardboard.

In 1993, in the cold, grey dawn, Molina Amandishe and her family were huddled round a small fire, all poorly dressed and the children barefoot. A harsh coughing racked the body of one small boy. Through a translator Molina described how drought, then the lack of money for seeds, food or school fees led her, six children and her 85-year-old mother to leave their village near Great Zimbabwe for Harare. Molina collects cardboard and papers to sell and eats bread out of dustbins. The family's only regular meal is lunch provided by the feeding centre at the nearby Anglican Cathedral.

Rose Chideme, the social worker running the Cathedral's feeding centre, said: "Last year we used to feed less than 100 people a day; now it is between 250 and 300 daily. This is certainly due to drought and to ESAP. What is noticeable is that we are getting many middle-aged people, especially men, now; it used to be only elderly people and children. Some of the men have indicated to me that they have lost their jobs due to ESAP."

Soaring prices, frozen wages

Under SAPs, poor people have to accept wage freezes while prices soar as inflation remains high, subsidies and price controls are lifted, and devaluation of their currency raises the cost of imports. Between 1979 and 1990 the capacity for feeding a family from the average Jamaican wage packet was halved. Wage restraint policies led to a drastic fall in real wages, while the removal of food subsidies and devaluation sent prices rocketing. Between 1970 and 1990 the price of rice in Jamaica soared by 1,900 per cent, flour by 2,100 per cent, and bread by a staggering 3,125 per cent.

Price hikes

Senegal faced a massive 50 per cent devaluation of its currency in January 1994. The price of imports, including foods and medicines, doubled immediately. This hit poor people hard, especially those in rural areas who spent over a third of their food bill on imported food, mainly rice. Industry was also hit by price hikes for imported inputs. Widespread unemployment is predicted.

Devaluation is supposed to encourage food production in Senegal, by making domestically produced foods cheaper than imports. But farming is very inefficient and needs more than price changes to revive it. Even after devaluation, Thai rice is still cheaper than the rice grown locally.

In Zimbabwe, prices went up by almost 50 per cent in the first two years of ESAP. Food prices rose faster, by over 70 per cent, and some key items by even more. The price of a bag of maize shot up three-fold in the 12 months to April 1992. In March 1993, the controls on bread prices were removed and the cost of bread shot up overnight from Z$1.63 to Z$2.20. Wages, meanwhile, lagged a long way behind.

Poor families are eating less. In rural Zimbabwe, Christine Sibanda and her family regularly used to eat eggs, bread, margarine, meat and fat cakes (a local speciality). Now, since her husband lost his job, they have bread only once a week or so, no fat cakes as flour is too expensive, and eggs and meat only very occasionally from their few livestock.

A backward step for women

"The situation of women will go back to what it was in the time of our mothers. It is regression for the women's movement", says Salina Mumbengegwi, a Christian Aid partner, describing the impact of ESAP in Zimbabwe.

When hardship is inflicted on a people, it is those with least power and most responsibility who suffer most. The World Bank has laid particular stress on the importance of education for girls as part of its strategy for helping a country's human resources grow. But in country after country, it is girls who are the first to be taken from school when fees are introduced, or uniforms become too expensive, or younger children need looking after so that their parents can earn a living. When food is short, it is more likely to be women and girls who get less to eat. It is women who are less likely to go to a clinic when health fees go up.

Logging, Agusan del Norte, Philippines.

ROMULO REGALADO

Women are the managers of poverty. In order to make ends meet, it is usually they who bear the burden by working longer hours. They may also have to cope with a partner who feels demoralised about his inability to provide when he has lost his job. It is women who have to improvise, perhaps by making goods at home that the family can no longer afford to buy on the market.

Sistren, a Jamaican organisation which Christian Aid supports, describes in its magazine how women have to do work which society considers unproductive, such as caring for sick and elderly relatives. But this work is actually a vital service in the face of government cuts in health. Many women cope by taking on two, three or four jobs at a time. Sistren says, "The bottom line is that the vast majority of our women are working very hard indeed to secure basic food, shelter and clothing for their families and themselves. Life, after all, must go on."

Environment: disappearing riches

SAPs are having a damaging impact on the environment of many Third World countries, especially on tropical forests and soil. In the Philippines, a concentration on growing export winners like bananas and asparagus is damaging the soil, as agricultural techniques must be chemical-intensive to meet global standards. Mangrove areas and shorelines are now being used for prawn production. Deforestation and degradation of the soil are becoming very serious problems.

Deforestation

A Friends of the Earth report published in 1993 draws on detailed case studies from Ghana, Guyana and the Philippines to show that structural adjustment is a major factor behind deforestation. In Bolivia, for example, increasing poverty and unemployment has driven people into the forest to clear land to raise cattle or grow soya.

Degradation of farming land

Environmental damage has also been caused by the increased production of crops for export, which the World Bank has encouraged. Small farmers in Zimbabwe have been encouraged to replace maize with tobacco, but tobacco depletes soil nutrients much faster than other crops, and rapidly destroys the viability of the soil.

In the Sahel region of West Africa, structural adjustment measures are damaging the capacity of land to produce food. Five Sahelian countries, including Senegal, have been urged by the World Bank to privatise common land that is suitable for growing irrigated rice. Rice has become a popular food in the Sahel: output has more than doubled in the last ten years. But the effect of privatising land has been to encourage unscrupulous merchants, looking for a quick profit, to develop rice fields without drainage. The result has been catastrophic. Rice grown on the banks of rivers in the Sahel stands in water which is very saline. This water has to be drained regularly and a new supply allowed in; otherwise, the salty water is left standing on the land for too long. When this happens, the water evaporates and a salt crust forms on the soil, making the land useless for agriculture.

Cheap irrigation schemes have now been built on thousands of hectares of Sahelian land, most of which has become degraded. But the cost of recovering land damaged by such practices could be so high as to make it uneconomic. Food growing land is in danger of being permanently lost.

Quality of life: the poor lose power

With widespread dispossession and migration, people are losing touch with their traditions and culture. They are also denied a voice in the structures controlling their lives. People are working longer and longer hours simply to keep their heads above water.

In Zimbabwe, hardship has led to alienation. Many, although not all, are resorting to individualistic strategies to cope, undermining a culture of mutual support. "Hopelessness has set in. People say: 'Oh ESAP, what can we do?' They have come to accept as normal having no jobs, no drugs in the hospitals, queuing for two hours to get a bus home. People no longer take control of their own lives," says Regis Mtutu of the Public Education Collective, an organisation supported by Christian Aid.

Lost lifestyles

When the mine where he worked closed, German Felipez had to migrate to another part of Bolivia where he now grows coca (used in cocaine) "on a patch of overgrown land". He misses the old way of life. "We had lots of social gatherings, and big fiestas, huge extended community, people arrived from all over to the mines, masses of people, then families, neighbours, friends, weekends, Carnival, August fiesta, New Year. Here it's a different atmosphere, a different climate, a different way of life. Everyone is busy looking out for how they are going to live, working dawn to dusk every day. You can't give freely of your time here."

Erosion of democracy and human rights

The World Bank has put increasing store by the importance of 'good governance', yet SAPs are actually undermining the ability of governments to govern. Democratically elected governments cannot make basic decisions, such as how much to tax the population, because the parameters have already been set in the SAP. Cutting government spending, whether it is on the military, basic services or infrastructure such as roads and bridges, is politically difficult and has left new democracies vulnerable.

CHRISTIAN AID/SALOMON CYTRYNOWICZ

The coca market in Villa 14 de Septiembre in Chapare, Bolivia.

The high price of protests

Many people believe that SAPs which are imposed have eroded their democratic rights. Protests against these programmes have led to riots, violence and even deaths. Demonstrations are becoming more frequent in Bolivia, with strikes, marches, road blocks and hunger strikes. Teachers have demonstrated against wage freezes, miners have focused on job losses and privatisation. The poor have mounted road blocks and marches against the abolition of food subsidies, lack of credit and trade liberalisation.

Human rights

People's most basic rights are being undermined. One of the tenets of the World Bank is that a country needs political stability to attract foreign investment. In Sri Lanka this meant the government opted for repression in order to force through some of the more severe economic reforms.

Sarath Fernando from the Devasarana Development Centre, an organisation in Sri Lanka supported by Christian Aid, has a wider perspective. He asks: "What about the human rights of people suffering malnutrition and increasing poverty, of farmers losing their land? There are very important human rights being violated here but they don't come under the World Bank's definition of human rights. It's a human rights issue when the fertiliser price increases suddenly and the children of the peasants have to go to school without breakfast."

Sithembiso Nyoni, director of ORAP, an organisation in Zimbabwe supported by Christian Aid, says: "Africa is going democratic, but ORAP is questioning the double standards in the West's attitude to this. The West welcomes us getting rid of dictators but it doesn't extend its belief in democracy to the economic policies it promotes in Africa, imposing its own model of development."

World Bank and IMF response

In the face of such evidence, why do the World Bank and the IMF continue with SAPs? For a number of reasons, they say. Both argue that the problems people face are symptoms not of SAPs, but of severe economic crisis, which is what SAPs are introduced to solve. So blaming SAPs for these problems is like saying ambulances are to blame for accidents, because you almost always see one next to a smashed car.

They claim countries which have not had SAPs, such as

Peru until recently, have had even worse social problems. And countries that did not invite in the World Bank or the IMF, such as Nicaragua during the 1980s, had to carry out the same sort of policies: finance ministers had very little choice.

Of course, SAPs have not caused all the problems of the Third World – things were already bad. But Christian Aid's charge is that the World Bank and the IMF have failed to make things better and for the poorest, have usually made things worse. Despite their poor record, the World Bank and the IMF fail to reassess their policies or allow countries to try their own solutions.

Gamini Corea, former Secretary General of the United Nations Conference on Trade and Development (UNCTAD), made the following comment to Christian Aid's Sri Lankan partners: "If a man has lost his job, the World Bank would no doubt sensibly advise him to cut back on cigarettes, eat cheaper food, and stop going to the cinema. But no amount of belt-tightening will get him back his job. For that you have to talk to the boss. In the world today, nobody is talking to the bosses."

CHAPTER 3

The human cost of World Banking

"They sit in judgement on governments, using their financial clout to influence economic policy in scores of developing countries."

(*The Economist,* October 12, 1991, on the World Bank and the IMF.)

Many countries are affected in similar ways by SAPs. This chapter will now look in more detail at how people in three countries – Zimbabwe, Bolivia and Sri Lanka – are being affected.

Zimbabwe

After a disagreement with the IMF in 1984, Zimbabwe put in place its own home-grown economic policies. It maintained fairly good rates of growth, while also improving health and education. But by 1990 there were problems: unemployment was rising rapidly; there was a chronic need for more foreign exchange; and world prices for Zimbabwe's chief exports – tobacco and cotton – had fallen. At the same time, the government was determined to continue repaying its foreign debt.

The only way to get the much-needed aid and foreign loans was to agree to a SAP, which the government duly did in 1991. It became known as the Economic Structural Adjustment Programme (ESAP). But ESAP failed to deal with the international factors which caused so many of Zimbabwe's problems, and instead called for the government to implement harsh austerity measures.

What has happened since has been so devastating that it is impossible to wait in a bus queue, talk to a shopkeeper or visit a village anywhere in the country without hearing people talking about ESAP. Few people know exactly what it is or why it was introduced, but they know all too well its impact on

Zimbabwe: Gladys and Samson Dube have started to raise chickens which they hope to sell for cash.

their lives and they are angry. The programme was soon given other names, such as 'Extreme Suffering for African People'.

The Zimbabwean government claims that ESAP is home-grown, but few people believe this, not least because it is the standard SAP package. This in itself raises the question: how sovereign is a government in the face of a foreign exchange shortage that can only be met with donor money?

ESAP has led to negative growth, spiralling inflation, a yawning gap between export earnings and import bills, and collapsing business confidence. In everyday terms this means that people are losing their jobs, they cannot afford basic food items or health care, and many children are being deprived of their education because parents cannot afford to pay the fees. Homelessness and crime are on the increase as people move to the cities in search of work which is not there.

Crime and punishment: the urban poor

Security companies are one of the few growth sectors in Zimbabwe, so much so that an organisation funded by Christian Aid helped a group of unemployed people set up the

ALARM Securities Co-operative in Harare. Even it was hit hard in 1993 by measures to combat inflation – a combination of interest rates which increased from 22 per cent to 33 per cent, and a credit squeeze, which reduced ALARM's overdraft limit.

Sixpence, a security guard with ALARM, is furious about ESAP. A fighter in Zimbabwe's struggle for independence, he now feels betrayed. "I fought for a country... which is good for the poor. I had hope. We all had hope. Well now look at this country. We fought for nothing. ESAP is the worst kind of animal killing poor people.

"This government is getting money from the western bloc; the British and Americans are giving the Zimbabwe government ideas. These things will not work here. People are getting desperate. That's why there is so much crime."

Bitter harvest: rural areas

Farmers and rural communities have not escaped the impact of ESAP. The drought was disastrous for them, completely wiping out crops and cattle in some areas. Families had to rely on relatives in towns and cities for food and money. When the drought ended, the first harvest was fairly good – enough for most people to feed their families – and villagers heaved sighs of relief, believing their problems would soon be over.

Then the reality of ESAP hit. Workers started losing their jobs, school fees were imposed, and food prices, far from going down to pre-drought levels, soared as subsidies were removed. Farmers did not have enough crops to sell, and most had used all their savings simply to get through the drought.

Maize is Zimbabwe's staple food, but seed has more than doubled in price. Government support for farmers has been drastically reduced, which in turn has affected food output. Ironically a 1989 World Bank report praised Zimbabwe for its agricultural policies. It pointed out that between 1979 and 1981, the government paid farmers 80 per cent more for their maize and that production tripled in the following five years. "The Zimbabwean experience shows that if... supportive agricultural services are available, smallholders will respond with increased production," said the report. But in 1991, under pressure from the World Bank, the government sharply reduced the farm supports that had been so effective.

Moffat and Christine Sibanda live in the Esigodini district, near Bulawayo, where Betty Mozira also lives. Moffat is 39, tall and slim and very friendly. He and Christine have three children. Sitting in their neat compound they described their despair when Moffat lost his job after 12 years as a lorry driver with the National Breweries of Zimbabwe. Orders were falling and then "the brewery told us that because of ESAP they would have to lay off people. I was worried but it still was a terrible shock when it happened."

Moffat was earning Z$505 a month and Christine was not working. His meagre savings were soon used up to pay the children's school fees. The couple have some land on which they grow maize, groundnuts, rape and melons, which was enough for their needs while Moffat was earning. Now, however, it is not enough. "I can't sell anything because the soil is not rich enough to grow a lot. I just try to feed my family. We can eat, and I collect firewood. But what about clothes and school fees?"

It costs money to even look for work, with bus fares into Bulawayo costing Z$15 return. Moffat says, "During the day I cultivate my land for two or three hours, then sometimes go and sit at the business centre to hear if there is any work going. I look for anything. I don't choose. I ask, but nothing is happening…"

Through a family unit association, organised by Christian Aid partner, ORAP, Christine now sells paraffin to other villages to bring in a little money. "I haven't bought clothes since my husband lost his job but I will soon need to. That is very expensive. Then there's the creche for the young baby. I send her so that I can help my husband collect firewood or other things."

It is not only the essentials of life which are hard to do without. In their living room hut was a battery-operated record player and a covered-up singles rack. Christine smiles sadly as she explains that they cannot use the record player any more because batteries are too expensive. One battery costs Z$30 and only lasts one month. "That's Z$360 a year," she says. "We need that money to eat and have clothes. But I miss it. I like music very much."

Barely managing: the middle classes

ESAP is affecting rural and urban communities, and all classes of society, including middle-class people such as managers, teachers and nurses.

Boniface and Miriam Moyo (not their real names) live in Chitungwiza, a satellite town of Harare. Before ESAP they lived comfortably on their joint salaries, had a well-furnished home, and ran a car. Boniface was a co-ordinator in the purchasing department of a shoe company, taking home Z$1,860 a year. Christine worked as a nurse in a private doctor's surgery. Disaster struck when Boniface was laid off and the surgery was burgled – a victim of the growing crime rate in Harare – forcing the doctor to close his practice.

Boniface's company had employed 358 people but had to cut the staff to 150. "It was because of ESAP things became difficult," claims Boniface. "First it was hard to borrow money because interest rates went up so quickly. People were not given enough time to prepare for ESAP, so not many firms were ready. Business became tough and we had to look at cutting costs. They trimmed the older and longer-serving members first – I'd been there 23 years. I feel bitter. We'd been told that ESAP would be a way of getting more investment into the country and more jobs. In fact, it is the reverse. ESAP was a nightmare to most of us, those who've lost their jobs."

Because he was under retirement age, Boniface only got 70 per cent of his company pension. They have had to sell their

Women from Christine Moyo's family unit work together to thatch the roof of a hut, built for a couple and their three children.

CHRISTIAN AID/GIDEON MENDEL

car, cut down on food, and Boniface now has to spend a lot of time at the communal lands at Mount Darwin, 193 kilometres away, growing sunflower and maize to sell. He is hopeful of getting another job but admits that at 47, his chances are slim.

Miriam is less optimistic, although she believes the doctor's surgery will re-open before too long. "Now that my husband and I are not working, it's worse for us," she says. "We buy less food as the cost is going up day by day. For breakfast we have porridge and sometimes tea. Lunch is *sadsa* [a maize dish] and vegetables. In the evening we eat sadsa and meat or beans."

Boniface says, "I rely very much on my children now. Three of them are working but one has had nothing since he left school."

In early 1992, the government started a Z$20 million Social Development Fund (SDF) as a safety net for those affected by ESAP. Families earning less than Z$200 a month should receive money from the SDF to help pay school and exam fees and to buy roller meal. The Ministry of Labour and Social Welfare, responsible for SDF, claimed that by mid-1993, 50,000 people had been helped, at a cost of Z$7 million. But few people seem to have heard of it or received any help from it. The Ministry's Permanent Secretary, Tendai Bare, admitted to Christian Aid that an awareness campaign about the SDF had "stopped through lack of funds".

Ms Bare conceded that "ESAP is a programme which is very harsh and is a bitter pill to swallow." But, she added, "there's no choice".

Others disagree. They argue that changes must be made. "ESAP is returning Zimbabwe to the 1970s," says Simbethiso Nyoni of Christian Aid's partner, ORAP. "The divide between rich and poor is growing. Independence was fought for to overcome the domination of whites over blacks; ESAP is the new colonialisation."

Perhaps the most telling comments about ESAP are found in the World Bank's own figures. Its 1992 World Development Report classified Zimbabwe among "middle-income economies"; its 1993 report classified the country, for the first time, among "low-income countries".

"Have you really understood that ESAP is killing us?"

(Christian Aid's Jessica Woodroffe visited Dema near Bulawayo in Zimbabwe and talked to Daisy Ncube about the impact of ESAP on her life.)

Sitting under the shade of the *msehla* tree chewing corn cobs, we were joined by five women dancing their way along the road, singing their greetings. Everyone fell silent when I asked about ESAP.

Daisy was the first to speak. "Here at Dema, ESAP is being fought. We don't want ESAP to find a home here and a wife here... Our problem is water – if it had rained, maybe we could have found strategies to counter ESAP."

"If there was no drought, would you still be suffering under ESAP?" I asked.

"Yes. Our suffering would be better, but we would still be suffering. We are going to make sure that ESAP does not penetrate our community. We are even prepared to work with other nations to overcome this problem. For us, ESAP is an alien coming to destroy our family unit, our way of life. We are taking a broom and sweeping ESAP out of our homes."

Asked how ESAP was affecting them, Daisy replied: "We have children at school; since ESAP we cannot afford to send them to school. Our development has gone back ten years. We were starting to save money; now we can't save any more. The value of money is less and we can only just afford the essentials. After independence we realised how behind we were, we needed to develop ourselves, but now ESAP comes in and stops us.

"It is not us but our children who suffer most. We don't see how we can survive... Any increase we might get in the price of food we sell does not balance the cost of the things we have to buy. It is not good enough to say ESAP may bring us things like electricity. That is not our priority. We are fighting for survival."

Another woman raised her voice in passion. "Our husbands have been retrenched [made redundant], our children have left school. We had managed to buy a flat in town where my husband stayed because he was working there. He was retrenched without any notice, we couldn't pay the mortgage so the flat was auctioned and we lost our investment.

"Not a single man in this family unit [five families] is now working. Most used to work in the gold mines, some in a bicycle factory."

Daisy finished by saying: "I get so angry talking about ESAP. My heart is bleeding." We fell silent for a while as though in mourning. Then gradually the cloud of ESAP lifted and Daisy's face brightened again. Again the teasing started, then the singing and finally the joyous dancing.

Bolivia

A corner of the main market in Cochabamba is crowded with young men from early in the morning. Many stay there throughout the day. They carry nothing, are poorly dressed and they mill aimlessly around, chatting in small groups or anxiously watching passing traffic. There is an air of waiting, of frustration, even desperation.

Cochabamba is Bolivia's third largest city, 2,600 metres above sea level in the Andean foothills. People come to the market if they want to hire casual labour for a day, a week, even a few hours. It could be loading or unloading, or work on building sites – mainly heavy, physical jobs. Indigenous women come to look for domestic work in rich households. Most prospective hirers offer derisory sums, as low as seven bolivianos a day (just over £1). But there are always plenty of people willing to accept anything, just so they can buy food that day.

Unemployment is high in Bolivia and there are no unemployment benefits. Thousands of jobs were lost as a direct result of Bolivia's SAP, which was put into effect in 1985 and led to a reduction in state institutions and the closure of mines and factories.

Enter the lenders

As early as 1956 the Bolivian government had received IMF help in return for curbing nationalisation and cutting social programmes. In 1985, Bolivia became one of the first countries to receive a structural adjustment loan from the World Bank.

Why did Bolivia need World Bank help? In August 1985, the newly elected government faced hyper-inflation, economic chaos and a debt crisis which made the country dependent on foreign creditors. So it made sweeping changes. The government introduced, by decree, a SAP that affected political as well as economic structures. This programme became known to millions of Bolivians by its title, Decree 21060, or simply the 21060.

Decree 21060 followed standard IMF/World Bank lines. Government spending was cut, especially by removing subsidies on food, fuel and transport, and by reducing social welfare spending. Wages were frozen and price controls scrapped. Trade was opened up and foreign investment

encouraged. And loans were made conditional on Bolivia privatising its 157 state-run enterprises. In 1986, Bolivia's foreign debt was rescheduled on favourable terms.

The decree transformed an economy that was previously dominated by the state. But among millions of the country's poor it caused outrage. And nine years later, they are still waiting for the benefits of the 21060.

What went wrong?

The main short-term objective of the SAP, reducing hyper-inflation, was successfully tackled. However, the drive to reduce inflation has carried a high price. It has not benefited the poor, as the spending power of the average Bolivian has continued to decline since the early 1980s. As specified by the Decree, wages were frozen. From 1985 to 1990, GNP per capita in Bolivia fell from US$630 to US$580. During the period 1987-91, the percentage of people living in poverty increased from 74.7 per cent to 80.1 per cent; in some rural areas, the figure may be as high as 97 per cent.

Unemployment: lost in the cities

One of the major casualties of the 21060 was Bolivia's mining industry – a serious blow, as tin was formerly Bolivia's major foreign exchange earner. Tens of thousands of miners lost their jobs when mines were closed down because of the impact of structural adjustment and the collapse in world tin prices.

Julio Cespedes, ex-miner who moved to the city in search of work.

CHRISTIAN AID/SALOMON CYTRYNOWICZ

Julio Cespedes is a gentle, articulate man who spent 15 years working in Bolivia's largest mine, Siglo XX. He is the son of a miner and was born in the close-knit Siglo XX community. It was there that his parents died. He describes what it was like there after 1985. "Every day 30 or 40 buses would leave Siglo XX. It was sad to see families divided, nephews and nieces one way, sons and daughters another. Now it is like a ghost town there."

Now that the mine has closed, Julio has to move to Cochabamba. He has no idea what he will do there. "I have no profession other than that of being a miner. The city is a part of our country, yet we do not know how to live in the city."

Nowadays, ex-miners are found in all the major towns and cities, selling goods on the street, hanging around waiting for work, doing anything they can to get by. Some, like Belisario Rojas, have tried to hang on to the only job they know.

Belisario is 28, and like Julio Cespedes, was born and brought up in a mining community. He recalls how full of life it was, with shops and even a good football team. Now most of the young people have left. Belisario and other ex-miners bought the rights to a mine the government was closing. They mine co-operatively but have very little machinery and are reduced to taking out the rocks by hand. He earns around £35 a month. His wife spends much of her day breaking rocks in search of low-grade ore. For this she earns around £12 a month. (It costs an estimated £24.30 a week to feed a family of six adequately in Bolivia.)

In turn, job losses in mining and other industries have led to a massive increase in the number of people working in the informal sector, more migration from rural to urban areas, and increases both in the number of people who grow crops for export, and in the those who grow coca for the cocaine industry.

Going to market

It is very difficult to walk down almost any street in or near the centre of any major town or city in Bolivia. Well over half the pavement is taken up with street vendors – some sitting on the ground, their wares spread on a plastic sheet in front of them, some with stalls, others selling from loaded wheelbarrows or trolleys. One street may be jammed with fruit and vegetable sellers, another with a row of electrical parts or toiletry stalls. In most places people are crammed side by side. Sometimes there are two rows on one pavement, with a small gap to channel pedestrians between them.

What is most incredible is that this is merely the spillover from the central marketplaces. City centres resemble one vast street market. It was not like that before 1985.

Julia Escobar is a tall, strong woman, aged 55, who has been a market vendor in Cochabamba since she was 12. Surrounded by piles of potatoes of different varieties, she describes how the growth in the informal sector has affected her. "There's far more competition now. You have to offer the lowest prices to have any hope of selling at all. Then it can be slow. Some days I end up selling at zero profit just to get some money to buy the daily bread."

However, she is defiant. "I've always been here. Never gone outside Cochabamba. And I'm not moving." In 1985 there were around 10,000 street and market vendors on the streets of Cochabamba. Today, probably one in five adults are vendors, with an estimated 35,000 vendors serving 580,000 people. Street traders come from all walks of life now.

Jonny Lopez and his wife both used to be professional teachers. They have a downtrodden air, as if they don't fit in.

Aymara stall holders in a street in La Paz, Bolivia.

CHRISTIAN AID/SEBASTIO SALGADO

"We both worked for eight years in the rural communities around Potosi (a mining community in the high Andes). Things got bad with the hyper-inflation in the 1980s, then the Decree 21060 came and it got worse. The price of food went up, wages did not. By 1985 we were earning 200 bolivianos a month each and half of that would go in fares to get into Potosí once a week to buy supplies. We simply couldn't live on it any more."

Jonny gave up teaching in 1986 and tried selling in the market at Potosi for four years, until the town emptied when the mines closed. He and his wife then moved to Cochabamba.

The lure of cocaine

The loss of markets and increase in imports caused by Decree 21060 has led to an increase in the numbers of farmers growing coca for the cocaine industry. In 1985 around 20,000 people grew coca in the Chapare region of Bolivia. Most coca in Bolivia is used for traditional, religious and legal purposes – in many rituals; more practically, it is also chewed to dull the appetite. Following Decree 21060, the number of growers soared to over 50,000 and more of the coca was used to manufacture cocaine for selling to the US and beyond. A harsh clampdown by the authorities, and coca substitution projects, have now halved that number. But coca growing and trading have attractions for people who are struggling to survive, even though they see none of the enormous profits.

One of the elements of Bolivia's SAP was the liberalisation of trade – that is, opening up the borders so that anything and everything can be imported without tariffs or restrictions, and without subsidy or protection for local produce or goods. This measure is having very real repercussions for peasant farmers, who, in trying to sell their small surplus, find that they are competing with Chilean tomatoes and Peruvian potatoes. The price eventually drops to a level where it is not worth taking the goods to market, which means that farmers cannot buy the oil, salt and soap for which they grew the surplus in the first place.

Diversification – and exploitation

Bolivia is attempting to increase its traditional export crops – cotton and sugar cane – and include others, such as sunflowers, with little or no regard for working conditions or environmental concerns. On land near Cochabamba, a 17,000-hectare estate is being converted to grow cash crops. The estate was recently bought by a Brazilian, and his mechanic nonchalantly explained that they would be clearing much more land the following year with heavy machinery smuggled in from Brazil. The crops, when harvested, will be transported into Brazil and then exported from there.

The SAP has left Bolivia completely open to the exploitation of its land and natural resources by foreign landowners. All Bolivia gets out of such activities is a small amount of export revenue and some poorly paid jobs with no security. Yet this is exactly the type of scheme supported within structural adjustment.

Orlando Rivadineira of the Federation of Salaried Agricultural Worker, estimates that in five to ten years' time, the whole of Bolivia's eastern lowlands will be cleared of trees – "peeled" is the word he uses – for export crops.

The search for work

The foreign-owned estates provide employment for thousands of men, like 18-year-old Teofilo Arancivil, who have left their homes to find work. Despite the poor pay and appalling conditions, there is no shortage of people flocking to the east, and wages are pushed even lower as labour becomes increasingly abundant each year.

Teofilo is from the countryside near Sucre, where his family have land on which they grow wheat, potatoes, fruit and vegetables. They had always used the surplus to buy what they could not supply themselves, such as oil and soap; but in recent years they have been unable to sell their surplus. As a result, Teofilo and his brothers have spent three to four months of every year living under tatty plastic in communal tents, working 12 hours a day under the searing sun.

Each day, Teofilo and 15 other men hack away at the remaining roots of trees cleared from the land, throwing any logs left by the machine onto the fire. They work from dawn, but will not complete even one hectare (2.5 acres) before it gets too dark to work.

The landowner pays US$45 for each hectare cleared. By the time the intermediary has taken his cut, Teofilo earns about £1.50 a day. He and the other migrant workers have to pay about five Bolivianos each for their food and board, leaving a total of three or four bolivianos to save each day (about £3 a week).

CHRISTIAN AID/CHRIS STEELE PERKINS

Festival of the Lettuce, Tacamar near Achacachi, Bolivia.

But soon Teofilo will not have even that meagre sum. Another intermediary has come in with a lower offer and his own list of willing labourers. He will pay them even less – and put Teofilo out of a job.

The Decree has also had a less tangible but decisive effect upon traditions of solidarity and mutual self-help. Increased poverty and the promotion of individual solutions have pitted people against each other in fierce competition for limited market opportunities. "In Bolivia, people's religious, social and cultural lives are completely interwoven," says Renato Pardo of CASDEL. Cultural disintegration, and particularly increased migration, is having a major impact on families and lives.

Stopgap solutions

The World Bank recognised from the start that Decree 21060 would hit the poor hard. To cushion the blow, the government of 1985, with help from the Bank, created a short-term fund to provide temporary employment for the very poor. The Social Emergency Fund (FSE) ran for four years from December 1986 and was later heralded by the Bank as a success story.

Managed by the private sector, the FSE created an estimated

19,000 temporary jobs, particularly in the building industry. But they could not compensate for the tens of thousands of jobs lost in the wake of the closure of state enterprises. The very poorest, most isolated communities had no access to the FSE, and many people were not even aware of its existence.

Most crucially, the FSE was never designed to deal with the long-term problems. The economic situation is still critical. The cocaine industry has reached saturation point. Street sellers cannot sell enough to live on. And peasant farmers, who in 1985 were still growing enough to send food to their relatives, are struggling to survive in the cities, and do not produce enough to feed themselves. Bolivia's output of export crops has risen since 1985, but its food crop output has fallen. According to the International Fund for Agricultural Development, Bolivia now has the highest level of rural poverty in the world. Yet in terms of annual income per head, there are 40 countries poorer than Bolivia.

The FSE was replaced by the Social Investment Fund, which has been more effective, as it has focused on health and education. But it remains part of the whole structural adjustment package and is inadequate for tackling the problems caused by the Decree.

After nine years of structural adjustment, 21060 are numbers the Bolivian poor would rather forget.

Sri Lanka

Since before the Second World War, the Sri Lankan government had given priority to raising the living standards of the poor. And it worked. Sri Lanka became internationally famous as a country where more children were at school, and where more people were able to read and write, get to health clinics they could afford, and expect to live longer.

Now the situation has changed. Malnutrition among children is increasing and many have been taken out of school to help their farmer parents who can no longer afford to hire labour. The Sri Lankan government's spending on health and education as a percentage of GNP is now below the Asian average. Yet the World Bank, challenged by Christian Aid on this record, talks only of reallocating health and education spending, not increasing it. For 17 years, structural adjustment policies have been in place, and poverty is at least as bad as it was at the start.

In 1977 a new government opened up the economy and cut back on social welfare programmes. An extensive programme of food subsidies was swept away. In 1988 the election of a new president forged even stronger links with the World Bank and IMF and in 1992 the most recent Enhanced Structural Adjustment Facility was ushered in.

A nation of farmers

Most Sri Lankans are farmers and the backbone of rural life is rice, or 'paddy', as it is known. The government traditionally supported it and as a result Sri Lanka produces about 85 per cent of the rice it needs.

But rice farmers have been hit by SAPs. The government removed a subsidy on fertiliser and the cost of farm inputs shot up. It cut back its crop-buying system and scaled down its advisory and training services to farmers. Farmers say that the government has also stopped supplying seeds for paddy, so they now have to buy low-quality but expensive seeds from private traders. As a result, the paddy price is stagnant or falling. In some districts, farmers are producing less rice than before and their income is falling. They believe the very culture of Sri Lankan life is threatened.

"My harvest doesn't cover the cost of production," says farmer Kamal Ranasinghe in the village of Yatawatte, some 25 miles from the town of Ibbagamuwa. "We used to grow two rice crops a year but we have stopped growing rice in the lean season because the income from paddy has decreased. We used to have agricultural extension [advice] services. Now there are only two advice centres left to over 200-odd villages. Farmers now have no one to turn to if they have a problem."

As one alternative, the government has encouraged farmers to grow more vegetables, such as tomatoes and onions. But encouraging the cultivation of more crops – standard World Bank advice – often means that too much of the same product goes on the market and so lowers prices.

In 1992 there was an enormous glut of tomatoes, and the price was rock-bottom. But as tomatoes, unlike rice, do not keep, farmers have to trade them after harvest in any case; they cannot wait for prices to climb up again.

For Bogaha Gedera Karunasena, a farmer in his twenties, married with two young sons, the tomato glut was the last straw. Already facing heavy debts, he could not face going on. He poisoned himself.

Karunasena, with his brothers and sisters-in-law, all depended on selling their tomatoes for a living. Although they all had a reasonable crop, they could not sell all of it. Karunasena had harvested 50 boxes of tomatoes (1,250 kilos) but only sold half for Rs 1.50-2 a kilo. This meant his income was less than Rs 1,250 – about £16.

"My son committed suicide because he was ruined," says Bobi, his mother. "It's as simple as that. He had taken out a lot of loans which he couldn't pay back because he couldn't sell his harvest."

Spiralling debts

Banks are getting tough with farmers who cannot repay, even though they followed government advice and are victims of economic circumstances beyond their control. In Polonnaruwa district, an organisation called the All Lanka Peasant Congress is spearheading the defence of farmers summoned for non-payment of loans. Its president, Kularatne Wickremasinghe, says that at least 75,000 farmers in Sri Lanka have been summoned for non-payment. He is annoyed that while the government has written off loans owed by large farmers and businessmen, it insists that small farmers repay. "It's one law for the rich and another for the poor," says Wickremasinghe.

Elinawathie Singho is among those who are being taken to court for non-payment of an agricultural loan. And she is reliving a nightmare – her husband committed suicide in 1986 because he could not afford to pay the very same debt. "We got into this mess because our income from paddy was not enough", she says. Elinawathie also grows tobacco on her three-acre plot – but her return from this crop in 1993 seemed unlikely to cover her costs.

For farmers, another alternative on offer is to grow one of the new export crops, such as gherkins. They, like tomatoes, may well be a useful extra crop for part of a peasant's field. But little of the land is suitable for such crops, and the international market for them is limited and fickle. As university lecturer Dr Piyasena Abeygunawardena puts it, "A hundred years of being the biggest tea exporter in the world did not enable Sri Lanka to puts its people on their feet. Does the Bank really think that 300 acres of gherkins will make a difference?"

Yet the World Bank seems determined to press on. In October 1993, its agricultural adviser addressed a World Bank seminar in Sri Lanka, calling for rice to be made less attractive, so that farmers will switch to more profitable crops. The import duty on rice should be removed, he said. Christian Aid's partners reject this analysis. Sri Lankan rice production is actually reasonably efficient, and it underpins the life of rural Sri Lanka. But there is cheaper rice available on the international market. Importing it freely would undermine the livelihoods of farmers in many parts of the country, including some of the poorest and most politically sensitive areas.

"We are going back to the colonial era," says the Rev Rienzie Perera, General Secretary of Sri Lanka's National Christian Council, an organisation supported by Christian Aid. He argues that SAPs are making the country more dependent and that the cost to people is high. He describes poverty and deprivation in the south of the country as dramatic. "Structural adjustment has led to widespread malnutrition, women skipping meals and feeling faint in the fields, children passing out in school assembly."

Precarious growth

Structural adjustment in Sri Lanka has succeeded in developing a new garment industry, with factories both in Export Processing Zones, and scattered over the country. But working conditions are often poor. In the medium term, the industry may well be unsustainable, either because northern countries deny access to Sri Lankan clothes, or because foreign investors can switch easily to another country, such as Vietnam, that offers even cheaper labour.

Meanwhile, no other new industry has been developed to any extent.

War

One great obstacle stands in the way of sustainable development in Sri Lanka – the war being fought in the north and east of the country. But structural adjustment has done nothing to promote peace. Indeed, some observers think that the inflow of nearly US$1,000 million per year of aid in support of structural adjustment has helped to prolong the war. Gamini Corea, the Sri Lankan former Secretary General of UNCTAD, took another line. "In the 1960s the Bank and the Fund were pressing Sri Lanka to abolish the rice subsidy. We said 'Sri Lanka is a peaceful, democratic country with no army to speak of, our food subsidies are our defence expenditure.'"

"Sri Lanka has changed from being a country with a relatively good quality of life," points out Sarath Fernando of a Christian Aid partner, the Devasarana Development Centre. While it is not possible to attribute a single cause, he says, "it is unavoidable to see the links between the process of change and the process of restructuring the economy according to the policies advocated by the World Bank and IMF".

It is clear that for the poor, and even the not-so-poor, in developing countries, SAPs are having devastating consequences for all aspects of their lives. Individuals have shared their stories in the hope that people in the richer countries can help them.

The World Bank and IMF are not evil institutions. Why then are they continuing to impose conditions which are destroying so many lives? Even by its own standards, the World Bank's policies are failing. What has gone wrong?

CHRISTIAN AID/MARTIN COTTINGHAM

Bicycle mechanic in his makeshift workshop, Kilinochchi, Sri Lanka.

CHAPTER 4

What went wrong?

The experiences of people throughout the Third World show us that SAPs are not working. They have not reduced poverty, and they have failed even when measured against the World Bank and IMF's own narrow criterion – economic growth. This chapter looks at why World Bank and IMF policies have failed and who controls them.

Economic growth – fact or fiction?

The destruction wrought by SAPs is not limited to a few isolated blunders. UNICEF pronounced SAPs in Africa a failure after documenting their widespread effects on health and education in its 1992 report. A decade's worth of SAPs has failed to reverse economic decline in sub-Saharan Africa; income per head is still falling and remains below 1970 levels according to the 1993 UNCTAD Annual Report.

The situation is not much better in Latin America. The Inter-American Development Bank, in its 1991 report, considered there to be no question that SAPs had exacerbated the problem of poverty in the region. Real wages have fallen while unemployment has increased across the continent. The 1980s saw a widening gap between rich and poor in countries under adjustment according to the UN Economic Commission for Latin America and the Caribbean.

The clearest evidence of the impact of SAPs on the economy, demonstrated by study after study, is that they have reduced investment. This is a damning indictment of a programme primarily designed to promote economic growth. Without investment there is no way an economy can return to sustained levels of economic growth.

Lessons of success

However, there are a few countries in South-East Asia and Latin America which have seen improvement in economic growth. They provide useful lessons but their applications are limited.

The success stories are all in larger, richer countries. Chile is a good example. It already had several factors in its favour: better natural resources, a stronger government structure and a better educated and trained population than most countries undergoing SAPs. The economy has grown well, but it depends very much on exporting products such as copper, whose price is at the mercy of international markets. There has been less success in improving services such as education or in reducing inequalities between rich and poor.

Where there are successes, they are as much to do with the level of aid given as with the impact of SAPs. Significantly, the high-growth countries of South-East Asia also had much greater government involvement than is prescribed under orthodox SAPs. Their experience is not easily translated, particularly to the poorest countries of sub-Saharan Africa who have weaker economies and less access to foreign investment and aid.

Small-scale industry in Chiang Mai, Thailand.

Why do SAPs not work?

SAPs were not designed to worsen the lives of the poor – quite the opposite. But as we have seen in country after country, their effect has often been to do just that. What has gone wrong?

Simple arithmetic

Part of the problem has arisen simply because the World Bank and IMF have practised bad economics. They failed to take all the factors into account and proposed policies which contradict each other. The most glaring example is the 'adding up' problem, where a large number of countries have all been told to increase their export of the same product at the same time, creating a glut and a subsequent slump in prices.

Peasant farmers in Ghana grow much of the cocoa used to make the chocolate eaten in Britain and Ireland. It is a useful cash-crop for farmers, as it can be grown alongside food crops. One in four Ghanaians are employed in growing and exporting cocoa, which provides 60 per cent of Ghana's export earnings. However, the World Bank has been encouraging several developing countries to grow and export more and more cocoa, as a way of earning money to service their foreign debts. This has helped to create a glut of cocoa, and the price on world markets has fallen by more than half in the last ten years. Now, cocoa-growing countries are having to run simply to stand still, and small farmers are getting less and less for their produce.

Conflicting aims

There has been conflict between the short-term goals of the IMF and the longer time framework of the World Bank's approach. Keeping interest rates high keeps down inflation but also reduces investment. Making imports more expensive has helped the balance of payments – but put up the import bill for domestic producers.

Understanding development

Economic growth is an important component of development – but the *type* of economic growth makes a crucial difference to whether or not the poor benefit. Where there is economic growth, it is often not leading to poverty reduction or improving the lives of the poorest.

The World Bank and IMF have not kept pace with the growing global understanding of the process of development. It is now recognised by most that poverty reduction is about more than just income: it is a complex issue which includes the need to give people control over their lives. Moreover, unless people are involved in the design of economic programmes, they are unlikely to work as intended.

One clear example of this is the failure on the part of the World Bank and the IMF to recognise that the different roles that men and women have affects the outcome of policy. Because women have less control over their lives, it is they who suffer most under SAPs. In most societies, men and women play different roles which are quite rigidly defined. The services previously provided by governments – like health care and schools – almost always have to be taken up by women, which increases their workload. At the same time, the fact that women may be the major income earners in a family unit is often ignored.

The switch from producing food to growing export crops, for example, often adversely affects women and therefore children. Women decide how to use the food produced, but the cash from export crops goes to the men.

Policies for the real world

One of SAPs' most serious flaws is that they do not take into account outside factors such as the prospects for trade, foreign investment and aid. Yet economic policy cannot be made in isolation from the real world. SAPs have also lacked realism about the non-economic factors which affect a country's development. Drought in Zimbabwe is the most striking example of this. SAPs come as a standard package with too few variations to cover adequately the vast differences between countries across three continents.

The World Bank and IMF often blame governments for the failure of SAPs. Some failures have certainly been due to the incompetence or corruption of Third World governments. Christian Aid does not absolve governments of their responsibility, but argues that the World Bank and IMF should take into account what governments are actually likely to do, and what it is politically possible for them to achieve.

A controversial package

There are political choices involved in coming up with these packages. Some would argue that SAPs follow a free market model which has not been proven to work anywhere – certainly not for the poor. The framework still used by the World Bank and IMF is similar to that followed in Britain and the USA in the 1980s – but without any unemployment benefits or social security. John Mihevc of the Canadian Inter-Church Coalition on Africa believes the World Bank is preaching a gospel of prosperity that provides a facile solution to Africa's crisis.

Doubts at the World Bank

World Bank economists have themselves acknowledged that luck plays a major factor in the success of SAPs. And within the World Bank there is a debate about whether they are effective at all. A report written by World Bank staff in 1992 concluded that adjustment lending in Africa had done little to help economic growth or inflation, and had actually contributed to a significant drop in investment. The report was initially titled 'Why structural adjustment has not succeeded in sub-Saharan Africa'; by the time it was officially released, the report's title had been changed to 'World Bank and adjustment lending and economic performance in sub-Saharan Africa in the 1980s'.

Altered approaches

The World Bank has begun to change its approach as a result of international criticism. Initially, it said little about poverty, for example. The Bank recognised that the economic changes needed might hurt the poor, and hoped this would be minimised. But it was not until the publication, in 1987, of a damning UNICEF study, 'Adjustment with a human face', that the World Bank began to talk about the need for a social component in adjustment programmes. It also began recommending social funds as a safety net for those most adversely affected.

In 1990, partly as a result of pressure from non-governmental organisations and other activists, the World Bank

went even further. It is now publicly committed to reducing poverty and most of its staff know the correct language to use.

According to the World Bank's 1993 report, its poverty reduction strategy is to promote a pattern of growth that enables the poor to participate through their labour. This means labour-intensive growth, combined with investment in people – such as spending on health and education – so that they can both contribute to growth, and reap its benefits. The report also acknowledged that safety nets should be provided for those who cannot work.

Rhetorical answers

But as we have seen earlier, the theory does not always work in practice. In many cases, unemployment has risen, while health and education levels have deteriorated. Safety nets are grafted on to SAPs as temporary shock absorbers. The need for such assistance is high, partly because of the failure of SAPs to bring about economic growth. But safety nets are consistently underfunded and governments lack the money to tell people how to claim benefits. And safety nets do not address the root causes of why people are poor.

Christian Aid welcomes the World Bank's change in approach, but judging by the evidence of individuals and partners in the Third World and the World Bank's own reports, the theory has not been translated into practice. The World Bank still does not recognise that its policies are contributing to poverty, not helping to solve it.

World Bank staff do, when pressed, acknowledge the mistakes they have made in the past but they argue that the organisation has changed. There are some examples of this. A recently produced assessment of poverty in Ghana is a study which shows more understanding of the complexity of the problem, above all because it was based on asking a cross-section of Ghanaians what they thought. There are a number of other participatory exercises that the Bank – although not the IMF – are promoting. But the basic principles of SAPs remain the same; the lessons learnt by the better staff at the World Bank are failing to permeate through to the economists who are really in control.

Mohammed Yunus is respected all over the world for his work on the Grameen Bank in Bangladesh, which has done a great deal to alleviate poverty. His view is that the World Bank has changed little. "Single-mindedly, it pursues growth...until it is distracted by other issues, like hunger, women, health, environment, etc. It adopts the rhetoric of all these issues pretty easily and quickly, but it cannot translate those rhetorics into action that easily."

Most recently, the World Bank's 1994 report, 'Adjustment in Africa', does little to reassure us that it really takes poverty seriously. The report evaluates governments' successes in putting SAPs in place, and draws the conclusion that those countries who have implemented SAPs have seen better growth. But the report itself admits that the growth rates of even the best performers in Africa are too low to reduce poverty by much in the next two or three decades. Despite all the research carried out, the best the report can come up with is that SAPs have 'probably' helped the poor – for which they provide no evidence. The authors are clearly 'true believers' in the free market model and can only offer the poor economic growth.

Who is in charge?

We have seen that World Bank policies are failing to reduce poverty, and in many cases failing even to produce economic growth. The World Bank, as a result of criticism, has shifted slightly in its approach to reducing poverty. But who has the clout to persuade the World Bank to tackle the root cause of the problem – SAPs themselves? Who controls the World Bank and the IMF? The answer, ultimately, is that we are supposed to be in control. It is our elected governments who are supposed to govern the World Bank and IMF.

Both organisations are controlled by a Board of Governors. Each member country is represented by a governor – but the number of votes each governor has depends on the financial contribution which the country makes. Rich countries therefore have more votes, and the industrialised nations hold the majority of votes. Day-to-day management of the World Bank is effectively left to the board of 24 Executive Directors. Five countries, including the UK, are guaranteed a seat on the Executive Board, while other countries have to share. So, for example, the Canadian Executive Director represents Ireland and much of the Caribbean. The IMF similarly has a Board of Executive Directors.

The UK, the World Bank and the IMF

The Chancellor of the Exchequer is the UK Governor for both the IMF and the World Bank. The Chancellor is accountable to Parliament for the money given to the two organisations, but there is almost no opportunity for debate. Contributions to the World Bank are discussed every three years in Parliament, when Parliament can only agree to or reject the proposed amount, not amend it. Technically, there could be a discussion in the Foreign Affairs Select Committee which would allow for a more in-depth debate, but this has never happened. Each year contributions to both the World Bank and IMF appear in a debate on the budget – but are not discussed.

Unlike the representatives of most other countries, the same person – a Treasury civil servant – is the UK Executive Director for both the World Bank and IMF. There is no opportunity for Parliament to debate his or her actions as the government's representative. Nor is there any evaluation of the extent to which the UK's contribution to the World Bank meets the objectives of its own aid programme.

John Denham MP, who is a member of Christian Aid's Board, recently wrote to the UK Executive Director asking him for a copy of a World Bank paper which was about to be discussed by the Board of Directors. He was told that the paper was confidential; ironically, the subject of the paper was access to information.

Parliamentary knowledge about the World Bank and IMF is altogether lacking. In March 1994 John Denham called a rare debate about the accountability of the World Bank. The debate was held at 4am and only two other MPs attended.

But an increasing number of MPs have expressed their concern about the lack of Parliamentary accountability. In a number of countries, including Canada, which has a very similar parliamentary system, successful campaigns have ensured that more debate occurs. Some MPs in the UK hope to achieve the same. In Ireland, a coalition of agencies is pressing for similar changes in the Dail.

Accountable to the UK

In the UK, Christian Aid is calling for:

- An annual report to Parliament and subsequent debate on
  (i) the role of the UK in the IMF and World Bank, including the voting record of the Executive Director; and
  (ii) an assessment of the efficiency and effectiveness of IMF and World Bank lending in relation to the British government's strategy for developing countries, which is outlined in the objectives of the Overseas Development Administration.

- Regular Select Committee hearings on the operations of the World Bank and IMF and the role of the UK Executive Director.

- Parliamentary Statements following the World Bank and IMF Annual and Spring Meetings. The Chancellor of the Exchequer and UK Executive Director should consider it their responsibility to alert Parliament if the wishes of the Board of Directors are not adequately carried out by staff of the World Bank and IMF.

- A discontinuation of UK government financing of the World Bank and IMF if it is not satisfied that substantial improvements have been made to ensure that the objective of poverty reduction is being fulfilled.

More say for the Third World

Ordinary people in the Third World have to live with the effects of World Bank and IMF policies, yet even their governments have little say about how the organisations are run. There needs to be much more consultation within countries. A veil of secrecy surrounds the work of the World Bank and even more so the IMF. Papers prepared by World Bank and IMF staff, which outline what is wrong with the economy and what needs changing, will not be made public, so people cannot comment on whether they agree with the analysis and prescriptions. Nor are the conditions attached to a loan made public, so affected people do not know whether the policies they disagree with are the responsibility of their government or the World Bank and IMF.

Access to information

In response to criticism there have been some welcome changes in the World Bank. A new information policy has been agreed. This is a step in the right direction, but much crucial information still remains confidential. The World Bank argues that this is because it is the property of the borrower government. Information tends to be made available after decisions are taken rather than before, when there is still time to influence the outcome. The World Bank has also set up an inspection panel which can judge whether the Bank has broken any of its own rules. Again, many of the proposals made by non-governmental organisations were not, however, adopted and critics of the Bank wait to see how independent the panel will be. Nevertheless, such moves should be applauded as steps in the right direction.

But there have been no such developments at the IMF. Information is very scarce and appears very late. There is no independent appeal mechanism. It should at the very least adopt information policies similar to the World Bank's.

A fair and open approach

Christian Aid is calling for changes to the World Bank and the IMF:

- Voting shares for countries represented on the Boards of Governors of the World Bank and the IMF should be changed so that poor countries are proportionately represented.

- New information policies should be approved which assume that information can be public unless there is a compelling reason to the contrary.

- Those affected by World Bank and IMF loans should participate in their conception, design and implementation.

- Independent evaluation of the impact of World Bank and IMF policies should take place. A list of internationally agreed criteria should be used, which go beyond economic indicators to include, for example, measures of poverty reduction, women's empowerment, health, and environmental sustainability.

Making staff accountable

The staff of both the World Bank and IMF pay insufficient attention to the Board of Governors. Staff have little responsibility for the mistakes they make. When the Board sets a policy – for example on poverty or on respect for the environment – there is no clear mechanism for judging whether staff follow it.

Inside the World Bank

The Financial Times, in a recent diary piece (October 20, 1993), noted the discrepancy between the World Bank's advice, and its own behaviour. Usually so strict on governments who exceed spending targets, the World Bank has overspent by nearly 50 per cent on its new Washington DC headquarters, which cost US$290 million. Meanwhile, Armeane Choksi, its Vice-President for Human Resources with responsibility for the World Bank's anti-poverty programme, gave us a taste of his lifestyle in a recent full-page advertisement for the sale of his house. It described lovingly the "luxurious master suite complete with jacuzzi, skylight, separate shower and circular windows, the grand first floor library with fireplace and the impressive entry foyer", not to mention "the dumb waiter which carries groceries direct into the kitchen".

Dr Michael Irwin, who joined the World Bank in April 1989 as director of its Health Services Department, resigned a year later "because I felt that the institution's activities were not really helping the many impoverished people in the developing world and also I was very concerned about its bloated, wasteful practices, its generally poor management and its unjustified arrogance".

In a speech in London, he claimed that the World Bank's travel costs came to about US$85 million a year, with staff flying first-class on journeys more than nine hours long. When he made a trip to East Africa, Irwin swapped his entitlement to a first-class seat to travel comfortably in business class, saving the World Bank US$1,900. This resulted in "considerable internal criticism", he stated. In December 1993 it was reported that World Bank staff would fly business class in future.

Of course, there are some dedicated World Bank officials who care very deeply and genuinely about poverty, such as Herman Daly. A long-standing World Bank employee, and senior economist of its Environmental Department until the end of 1993, Daly has won international recognition for his writings on the social and environmental aspects of economics.

On leaving his job to take up a university post, Herman Daly said that it had been a "high privilege" to "green the Bank's economists". But he blasted its "culture of secrecy", and said it needed "eye glasses and a hearing aid to improve interactions

It is clear that the World Bank and IMF should be made to listen – but what would we say to them? The next chapter will look at why their approach to poverty and economic change is

with the external world". He attacked the World Bank's top-down management which, "misguided by an unrealistic vision of development… has led to many external failures". Calling for more openness, Daly said, "there is really not much to hide and it is important not to hide those things it would be tempting to hide".

When Christian Aid's Jessica Woodroffe spent a month working on a secondment at the World Bank, what struck her most was the seeming arrogance of many of the staff. "They firmly believe they know how to run a country better than that country's elected government and the people who live there, even if they have only briefly visited it themselves", she says. "Their attitude to governments and NGOs alike is patronising. Some staff have incredible power and influence over the lives of millions, yet they are almost never fired for their mistakes. They don't see themselves as answerable to the electorate of the governments who fund them, and do not feel the need to carry out the wishes of the Board. There are good members of staff, but their voices are lost in the clamour of complacency and self-congratulation."

fundamentally flawed and will consider alternative methods of economic reform, and the kind of alternative goals which people would put forward if they had a chance to speak.

CHAPTER 5

Alternatives

"Standard structural adjustment programmes are essentially anti-poor and anti-growth. The record of structural adjustment programmes in the Philippines speaks for itself. These programmes have always resulted in worsening poverty and economic slow-down, if not decline." (Freedom from Debt Coalition, Christian Aid partner in the Philippines)

The World Bank and the IMF have a global plan for development, which includes SAPs. Christian Aid does not have a similarly detailed alternative to offer. What we can show is how SAPs could be improved, and offer some principles from which any alternative should be built. This chapter will also look at some examples of how these principles are applied at the local level in countries such as Zimbabwe.

When faced with their record of disasters, World Bank staff tend to respond by saying that things would have been worse without SAPs. This is not good enough. Change was desperately needed – but not this sort. SAPs can be improved, but more fundamental changes are also needed if the lives of the poor are really to change.

Tailoring SAPs to fit

There is no single alternative to SAPs. Really listening to people means hearing a variety of different answers, each of which best suits a different community, economy or problem. The result will be a new vision of development with a set of goals very different from those of the World Bank and IMF and a set of policies suited to each set of goals and circumstances.

Many of the common problems emerging again and again in countries implementing SAPs could be avoided. The World Bank and the IMF need to adopt a more pragmatic, case-by-case approach to economic policy-making, tackling areas such as trade, the role of government and working conditions.

The tobacco auction lines at the Tobacco Sales Floor in Harare, Zimbabwe. Every day 17,000 bales of tobacco are sold in five separate auction lines.

CHRISTIAN AID/GIDEON MENDEL

Trade: an eye to the market

The advice given to most countries is that they should export more goods, usually commodities like cocoa or coffee, so that they can earn more money to pay for their development. We have seen that gluts occur when several countries do so at the same time.

The kind of exports which are being promoted should change from commodities, where prices are tending to fall, to processed goods which hold their price better. Countries also need to diversify the products they sell abroad, so that they do not have to rely on just one or two, and consequently are not so vulnerable to falls in price. Trade among countries in the same region is also an important way forward, yet most SAPs discourage this.

Governments: a complementary role

SAPs are set on reducing the role of governments. Governments have not always played a beneficial role: many are both undemocratic and inefficient. But there is a demonstrated need for 'good' state intervention in the development process. The newly industrialised countries, such as South Korea or Taiwan, are prime examples of the necessary roles of the state in achieving economic growth, for example, in protecting infant industries, steering industry or collecting taxes. There is even more need for government intervention if development is to achieve 'non-economic' goals like the redistribution of resources from rich to poor and improving the position of women. A more objective consideration is needed of the actual strengths and weaknesses of both the state and markets in each country.

Banishing barriers to investment

Economic growth requires investment. But both the IMF and World Bank are preoccupied with reducing inflation by keeping interest rates high. But high interest rates have forced many small enterprises out of business. And few will invest in new businesses when, because of SAPs, people have very little spare cash to buy anything. SAPs should deal with the barriers holding back private investment, such as high interest rates, low domestic demand and weak infrastructure. This, in turn, suggests the need for a greater, not reduced role for the state in providing, for example, infrastructure and credit for low income groups.

Access to land, tools and credit

The World Bank poverty reduction strategy aims to help the rural poor by increasing the prices of certain crops. Farmers who sell these crops will benefit, particularly if they can increase the amount they produce. However, poor farmers with little land, few tools and no credit to buy fertiliser cannot expand their production or switch to growing a different crop. The truth is that most poor farmers do not gain. This is particularly true for many women farmers. If the poor really are to benefit from economic growth, they must have land, tools and credit. Land reform measures, for example, mean that farmers can finally own the land their families have farmed for decades. As well as being just, this provides them with an incentive to farm in a sustainable way so that the land is still productive for their children.

The right to borrow

Credit facilities are needed so that those without any security to offer against a loan can borrow money. In Bangladesh there are many such schemes, like the Grameen Bank and Christian Aid partner, HADS (Humanitarian Agency for Development Services), where groups of borrowers are helped to use loans wisely and meet repayments. The loans enable farmers to buy seeds, bicycles and farming equipment.

Getting it right for women

In all countries there are economic, political and social barriers which discriminate against women. If development policies are to succeed for all the population then they have to address these inequalities. Instead, many World Bank and IMF policies are 'gender blind', failing to see that men's and women's needs are not always the same. All economic programmes should consider the effect that they will have on women as well as men. Policy-makers need to discuss plans with women as well as the traditionally male representatives of a community. Moreover, women's needs have to be met not just because hurting them will hurt their children, but because they too have rights.

Washing plastic rubbish for recycling in Zimbabwe.

CHRISTIAN AID/GIDEON MENDEL

Many SAPs actually make the situation of women worse because they focus on money and the market; much of the work done by women is unpaid, and therefore not recognised. SAPs have tended to assume that women's time is infinite. Government services can be cut only because women become unpaid nurses and teachers and child minders and spend longer finding cheap food or walking because transport is too expensive. Because it is men rather than women who are seen (often wrongly) as the 'breadwinners' of the household, it is women who are fired first when jobs are lost or girls who are removed from school when fees are introduced. Before it is agreed, the particular effect of every economic programme on women as well as on men should be considered to ensure that unequal burden most women have to bear is not further increased.

Fair working conditions

The World Bank poverty reduction strategy assumes that the poor will benefit from the fruits of economic growth if that growth occurs in industries which employ large numbers of people. But often the only way that Third World industries can be competitive is by paying very low wages under appalling working conditions.

Legislation on minimum wages, labour conditions and environmental protection should not be suspended in order to attract foreign investment. As we have seen, this is all too often the case under SAPs.

Protecting social services

Horace Levy of the Social Action Centre in Jamaica, a Christian Aid partner, believes that no SAP should be accepted if it lowers the standard of health, education, wages and other social services below a minimum level.

More importantly, the World Bank should not design a programme which is going to make the lives of the poorest worse. Until the world community agrees to change economic conditions on an international scale, adjusting to these conditions will hurt. But it does not have to hurt the poorest. Central to the World Bank's poverty reduction strategy is Human Resource Development – investment in the health and education of the population. Yet in most countries with a SAP, health and education services are deteriorating, particularly for

THE NUTCRACKERS..!

the poorest who are unable to pay the ever-more-prevalent fees. Through consultation, economic policies should be redesigned so that they reduce poverty, rather than focusing narrowly on economic growth.

Changing the fundamentals

While SAPs can be improved, fundamental changes to World Bank and IMF thinking are needed if real change for the poor is to result.

More democratic

The World Bank and the IMF have consistently failed to consult the people they are supposed to be helping. These are the people who know how their country works, who have to implement the policies, and who must ultimately have the right to say what kind of development they want in their country.

This brings us to the heart of the matter. There is never just one economic solution to a problem. The economic 'advice' provided by the World Bank and the IMF is not just objective, technical advice. It involves political choices; choices about where a country should be going, how it should get there, and who should pay the cost.

Africa is one of the chief victims of the World Bank's failure to listen. In 1980, African leaders and UN aid agencies met in Nigeria and agreed the 'Lagos plan of action for the economic development of Africa, 1980-2000'. It speaks of the need for Africa to achieve a greater degree of self-sufficiency. Disregarding the publication of this report, the World Bank went ahead and produced its own plan for Africa the following year. The plan, according to Adebayo Adedeji, Executive-Secretary of the UN Economic Commission for Africa in 1980, and the Lagos plan's chief author, "turned out to be the very antithesis of the Lagos plan", recommending that higher prices be paid to farmers for export crops. "Even if export crop output were to grow at the expense of food crop production, it is not necessarily bad", it said. African leaders felt unable to reject the World Bank plan in case their own loan applications were then rejected.

Some World Bank officials now acknowledge that a different approach is needed. Referring to the imposition of adjustment programmes in Africa, Edward Jaycox, the World Bank's Vice-President for Africa, said in 1993: "We are now insisting that the governments generate their own economic reform plans. We'll help, we'll critique, we'll eventually negotiate and we'll support financially those things which seem to be reasonably making sense, but we're not going to write these plans. We're not going to do this any more." Sadly, this is not a view representative of the World Bank, and even less the IMF.

Given the failure of IMF and World Bank policy-making to bring about sustainable development, surely it is time for them to take a less conceited stance and allow countries to develop their own strategies. This does not mean training a country's economic managers in the World Bank or IMF and then approving the standard SAP they propose; it means really being flexible about country-specific programmes. Where there are conditions attached to loans, these should refer to outcomes affecting poverty – like infant mortality or primary school attendance – not specific macro-economic policies like the level of interest rates.

Some governments, too, do not listen to their people. What is needed are societies where broad-based debate is encouraged. It is vital that the World Bank and the IMF support such a process and submit their own proposals to such scrutiny.

Global problems

Too many of the costs of global economic problems are currently borne by people in the Third World. There should be a more equal sharing of the costs of these problems. It is no good one country trying to put its house in order in the face of problems which are international. If Third World countries are really to have a chance, there will have to be a redistribution of resources from North to South.

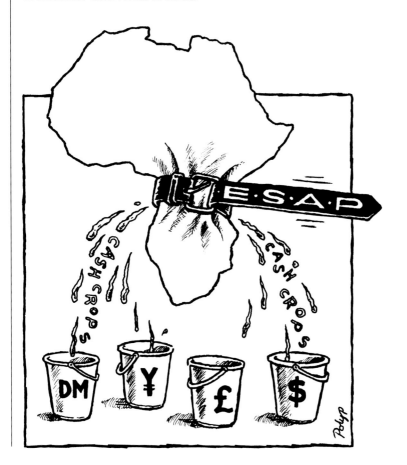

Some World Bank staff argue that it is 'external' factors like falling commodity prices and continuing debt repayments which are preventing SAPs from leading to the kind of developments they were supposed to provide. Christian Aid agrees, but this was entirely predictable. World Bank economists should take the real world into account when designing SAPs. It is no good developing an economic programme which will work in theory, if it ignores what is happening outside the country.

Redistribution of wealth

The diagram (below) shows the World Bank's projections for average incomes in rich and poor countries in the next 40 years. The market, it seems, will create a much-widened gap: only deliberate international policies would create a fairer sharing out of the world's wealth. That would not in itself guarantee that southern governments would act to increase the incomes of their peoples, but it would give them the opportunity to do so, instead of the present necessity to cut back.

Towards fairer trade

One clear example of ignoring what is happening in the real world is unfair trade. Third World countries are trying to export more, but protectionism in the North prevents them. For

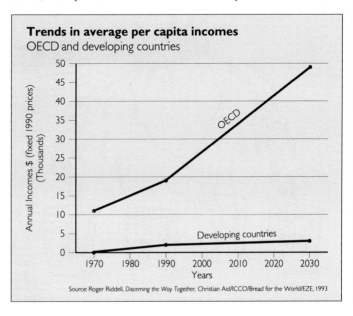

Trends in average per capita incomes
OECD and developing countries

Source: Roger Riddell, *Discerning the Way Together*, Christian Aid/ICCO/Bread for the World/EZE, 1993

people in the Third World to have a chance, rich countries in the North must be persuaded to remove barriers against imports from the Third World, particularly for processed products like textiles or canned food. The practice of dumping subsidised European agricultural products in African countries and undercutting local food production should be also stopped. Global controls are needed on transnational corporations to prevent them from sidestepping national regulations. And the Bank should support regional trading arrangements, to help countries specialise and produce goods that their neighbours want.

A way out of debt

In its 1994 report on Africa, the World Bank notes that debt is a serious obstacle to growth in most of Africa and that additional debt relief is necessary. Many governments have to use precious resources to repay governments and companies in the North at a time when the World Bank and IMF are telling them to cut their expenditure.

Yet, unlike most governments, the World Bank and IMF refuse to reduce the debt owed to them by the poorest countries, and insist they pay on time. As a result, debt owed to international institutions has become an increasing problem. In 1993, nearly one-seventh of all outstanding debt was owed to multilateral organisations like the World Bank and IMF, and the proportion is gradually increasing. Particularly for the most indebted, poorest countries, the proportion of debt-servicing which goes to these institutions is much higher, nearly 40 per cent – the actual amount increased from US$3 billion in 1980 to US$17 billion in 1992. As a result, the Bank and IMF, together with the smaller multilateral agencies, actually received in repayments as much as they loaned to the Third World between 1987 and 1992. Third World debt-servicing to the multilateral agencies was US$36 billion in 1992. By 1999 it will be US$50 billion if nothing is done. The World Bank and IMF should reduce the debt repayments they claim and should also support measures to reduce debt owed by Third World countries to governments and banks. It is no longer credible for the World Bank or the IMF to claim that they cannot cancel debts. Numerous options have been put forward, not least from the UK Chancellor of the Exchequer who suggested that the IMF could sell off some of its gold reserves.

An alternative vision of development

The World Bank and IMF vision of development is different from that of Christian Aid and its partners. Whatever the rhetoric, the bottom line for the World Bank and IMF remains economic growth.

Christian Aid believes the goals of any economic programme must be decided by the people who are supposed to benefit, particularly when they will be expected to bear the costs of transition. Instead the World Bank and IMF impose standard packages of reforms on countries with completely different cultures and societies. If the World Bank and IMF really listened, they would have to change their tune.

Christian Aid and many of its partners believe that World Bank and IMF definitions of development are inadequate. Christian Aid's vision is of a style of development in which people matter and are trusted, and are treated as though they count. Where people participate in decisions which affect them and where the quality of life is more important than economic growth. It is a vision of people sharing and learning together, where everyone's contribution is valued, where people can meet their needs. It is a vision of a just society.

Silveira House, a Jesuit organisation in Zimbabwe, stresses: "The alternative strategy to ESAP is a development of the people, by the people, for the people, based on equity and social justice, meeting basic needs, protecting the environment, alleviating poverty and integrating all the people."

Putting the poor first

The World Bank and the IMF believe that the benefits of growth will eventually trickle down to the poorest. Christian Aid's view of development is the opposite – putting people first, and the poor first of all. Economic growth is needed in the South, but it has to be a type of economic growth which increases both the income and the quality of life of the poor. "Material wealth is valuable only in enabling us to achieve what we really want from life", says Christian Aid's Jessica Woodroffe after visiting Zimbabwe. And she cautions, "By taking us further from those values of solidarity and happiness, economic development can undermine the very goals it should be trying to achieve. Maize is important – but so is dancing."

Culture and tradition are crucial for people's development.

Rigoberta Menchu, the Guatemalan indigenous leader and 1992 Nobel Peace Prize laureate, says: "We defend our roots, not only to defend them, but that they may flourish and bear fruit. We defend our roots as the foundation of development. We seek to protect our roots, so as to pour all the richness of indigenous values and original thinking into a new concept of development."

Rigoberta Menchu, winner of the 1992 Nobel Peace Prize.

WCC/PETER WILLIAMS

An alternative market

Some shoppers in the UK are already using their purchasing power to help farmers in the Third World earn more for their produce. This is partly thanks to Christian Aid's **Trade for Change** campaign, which aimed to increase demand and get fairly traded goods onto supermarket shelves. A promising start has been made, with all major British supermarkets stocking cafédirect, a fairly traded filter coffee. Sainsbury's and Tesco have started selling fairly traded chocolate, Maya Gold.

Products like cafédirect and Maya Gold give producers a better price for their crops than they can get on the world market, which is heavily weighted in favour of the richer nations. Because the free market decides how much of a product is produced and at what price it is sold, the producers of products such as cocoa or coffee have no say. They simply have to accept whatever price rules. And when the world price collapses, they cannot produce enough to make a living.

In 1991, four alternative trading organisations (ATOs) – Oxfam Trading, Traidcraft, Twin Trading and Equal Exchange – came together to buy a high-quality coffee direct from over 20,000

Shoppers in Oxford buy cafédirect at the Co-op.

CHRISTIAN AID/ELAINE DUIGENAN

coffee producers in Mexico and Costa Rica. Working on small family farms, the farmers have formed associations and co-operatives to improve their own conditions and to make direct export possible. Like other coffee growers, they have been affected by the recent steep decline in world coffee prices. Selling their crop at a higher price to the ATOs' cafédirect project provides them with income and cuts out the middlemen. Higher incomes mean that families can improve their transport, buy agricultural equipment and make improvements in the community. It means they have more control over their own lives.

Justino Peck is a cocoa farmer in San José village in Belize, Central America. He, his wife and their three young children made a comfortable living from selling cocoa beans, a traditional crop for the Maya people in Belize. The cocoa farmers were encouraged to produce more, and Justino was doing so well he decided to build a new roof for his house.

Then, in 1986, the price of cocoa began to fall dramatically. (It fell from £2,425 per tonne in 1984 to £610 per tonne in 1992.) It was not even worth the farmers harvesting the ripened crop, so they let it rot. Justino bitterly regretted the cost of the new roof. In an effort to help themselves, the farmers set up an organisation so they could collectively transport and market their crop, so cutting down their costs. The Toledo Cocoa Growers' Association (TCGA) elected Justino chairman and arranged a loan so that it could pay the farmers when they delivered their cocoa, to keep costs down and to encourage the farmers to at least pick what they had. But with the price of cocoa so low, it failed to attract many farmers and the Association soon fell behind on its regular loan repayments.

Then, out of the blue, says Justino, "we were approached by Green & Black's chocolate company who wanted to buy cocoa from us". Seeking the Fair Trade Mark, Green & Black's offered the farmers well above the market price, at 48p per pound, with a three-year guarantee to buy all they could produce.

"Now at last we can make plans for the future," says Justino. "One thing we intend to do is to improve the road from the village to make transportation of the cocoa easier and more efficient."

The farmers in Belize are better off, and British shoppers can now buy the delicious Maya Gold chocolate. It is the first product to receive the Fair Trade Mark, a recognition that a product is traded fairly. The Fair Trade Mark is an initiative of the Fair Trade Foundation, which Christian Aid helped set up.

Partnership in action

Christian Aid's partner organisations are showing at the local level the alternative principles that need to be applied nationally and internationally.

Small is beautiful

Brazil, one of the world's most heavily indebted countries, turned to exporting in a big way to pay its debts. Huge estates have been given over to growing crops for export, causing considerable disruption to the lives of millions of Brazilians.

The Agrarian Foundation of Tochantins-Agraguaia (FATA) was founded in 1988 by four rural workers' unions in Maraba, in the northern state of Para. FATA, an organisation supported by Christian Aid, promotes an alternative strategy of development in the eastern Amazon region. In particular, it is helping to develop sustainable alternatives for small-scale farmers who lack resources. The immediate target group for its work are 12,000-15,000 peasant families out of a total of 60,000-75,000 in the area.

FATA offers more than a service to its target group. It involves them in their own organisations, so that they can participate fully. With support from Christian Aid and other agencies, it has built a research and training complex, where courses are held and research carried out into matters of interest to small-scale farmers. And FATA has developed an alternative strategy for marketing rice which avoids the traditional middlemen, and which has led to the creation of a small farmers co-operative.

FATA's work shows people in the Amazon that agriculture does not have to be large-scale and export-orientated. It provides a vision of a way of development in which the poor are involved.

Working together

In Zimbabwe, Christian Aid's partner, the Organisation of Rural Associations for Progress (ORAP), has fiercely resisted the values that structural adjustment has tried to impose. Set up in March 1981 by a small group of people in Matebeleland who came together to discuss development options, ORAP stresses the need for people to act and work together in a truly democratic manner. It has grown fast; by February 1991,

CHRISTIAN AID/GIDEON MENDELL

Blacksmiths' workshop for training and sharing of traditional skills, organised by ORAP.

membership was over a million in some 800 village groups, making it the largest organisation of its kind in southern Africa.

ORAP members work in groups at different levels. The basic unit is the extended family of five to ten families, involved in domestic and craft activities, both to use at home and to sell. The next level of organisation, the village group, comprises several extended families and undertakes small-scale community projects, such as building dams and wells, preserving indigenous seeds and trees, and engaging in economic activities such as working the grinding mills, fattening cattle and raising pigs. Most jobs are done collectively – fetching water and firewood, for example, and tasks such as home improvements, which have been extensive, despite the squeeze on incomes caused by ESAP.

The basis of ORAP's work lies in a Zimbabwean tradition of collective work known as *analima,* whereby all group members attend to each family's needs in rotation. At a district level, associations also run economic programmes; some have their own development centre which gives training in agricultural, industrial and craft skills. ORAP also runs a traditional medicines programme which seeks to revive the knowledge of healing herbs that are available locally. It encourages sustainable agricultural methods that use indigenous crop varieties and natural manures.

In 1993, ORAP won international recognition for its work when it received the Right Livelihood Award, the alternative Nobel Prize, "for motivating its million members to choose their own development path according to their culture and traditions".

Learning from the past

CIPE is an organisation supported by Christian Aid which works with peasant communities in the impoverished department (county) of Potosí in Bolivia. Its alternative vision is the adaptation of traditional economic and political structures to modern society.

The *ayllu* is the traditional form of Bolivian community organisation. Within the *ayllu* there are different types of land use, including community control, inter-community control, and private family use. The most prominent form is a system of jointly organised production rotation. The *ayllu* has managed to survive in parts of the country despite Spanish colonialism, independence, the introduction of modern political parties, and more recently, the ravages of drought, floods and structural adjustment.

In Potosí, the *ayllu* remains strong and CIPE is helping to build on and improve it. Potosí covers different micro-climates, ranging from the high Andean plain to the warmer, more fertile valleys. By working collectively, the farmers in Potosí are not dependent on just one crop but can diversify to make the most of each different type of land and climate. CIPE helps with jointly organised crop rotation systems and the production of indigenous grains and potato varieties which are suited to the windswept, barren plains. And it works to strengthen systems of barter which have kept the *ayllu* alive for over 500 years.

"We are not interested in creating a living museum," says CIPE worker Alex, "but rather promoting an alternative to an economic model which sees so many people as superfluous to its needs. The peasants here know their environment; we want to give them the confidence to use that knowledge."

And it is working. A Christian Aid project officer visited one community, Antacucho, in early 1994, shortly after the region's potato crop had been devastated by frosts and hail. Plot after

Burning peat to protect the crop from frost.

plot of flowering plants lay burnt and bedraggled. But in Antacucho the plants stood a metre high, flowering and healthy. "We brought down peat from the spring", explained Francisco, one of the farmers, pointing to a verdant patch on the hillside. "When we'd dried it out, we mixed it with used motor oil, put it in tin cans, and placed them strategically on the plot. When the first frost came we rose in the middle of the night, and lit the tins. The smoke acted as a blanket and saved our crops. Our ancestors knew the technique but we had lost it. It will help the community to survive."

Better ways forward

People in developing countries are refusing to accept that outsiders know what is best for them. Often drawing on traditions, they are finding new ways of developing that feel right to them. People are organising themselves to get a better deal out of the wreckage that structural adjustment has caused, and are working for a world where the poorest matter.

CHRISTIAN AID/SEBASTIO SELGADO

CHAPTER 6

Fighting back

"The plain fact is that we are starving people, not deliberately in the sense that we want them to die, but wilfully in the sense that we prefer their death to our own inconvenience."

(Victor Gollancz, War on Want)

The World Bank and the IMF do not set out to harm the poor. But their view of development does not meet the needs and aspirations of people who are powerless in the face of poverty. As this book has shown, there are alternative visions which reflect people's goals, both economic and social, which should be recognised. There is no single vision as each community will have its own, but there will be common themes of people-friendly development.

The roles of the World Bank and the IMF are to provide funds and advise on policies which help countries meet these goals. This means that both institutions must fundamentally rethink the economic policies they have been advocating and show more willingness to explore the alternatives.

The UK and Ireland are two of the countries from all over the world whose government sits on the Board of Governors of the World Bank and the IMF. Christian Aid believes that these member governments have a responsibility to ensure that lending by the World Bank and IMF furthers people-friendly goals. In turn, the World Bank and the IMF need to be made more accountable to governments and people for judgement about whether they succeed or fail.

The World Bank, IMF and member governments should also work towards creating a better climate in which people-friendly development can take place. To begin with, the debt crisis and unfair trading system need to be tackled.

Ordinary people in the South and North are now taking action to force change on the World Bank and the IMF. This chapter will look at action on a local and international level, including Christian Aid's own recommendations for change. It will also consider the key role that people in Britain can play in this process of change.

Taking a stand locally

On February 8, 1994 the city of Cagayan de Oro on the island of Mindanao in the Philippines was brought to a halt. Six major barricades blocked key roads and spontaneous barricades were erected all over the city, built from stones, trees, tyres, cans – anything that was to hand. Ninety per cent of the population was involved. It was the first time the people of Cagayan de Oro had taken to the streets.

The issue was a levy on the price of oil, implemented by the Filipino government as part of its attempt to win the approval of the IMF for a new loan. Raising the price of oil appears to have advantages – it is beneficial for the environment, and hits car owners more than the poor. But for the people of the Philippines it was the last straw. In January, the day after the IMF team left the Philippines, the increase in oil prices was translated into a steep rise in the price of basic goods, bus fares and electricity.

Norma Acudili was one of those speaking at the rally in Cagayan de Oro. She is one of the many Filipina women campaigning for change. Norma lives with her husband and

Industrial development, Mindanao, Philippines.

CHRISTIAN AID/DERRICK KNIGHT

four children in a wooden house in a densely packed area just off the main road. Mud tracks separate the shacks, many of which are on stilts above stagnant pools.

With the help of Movement for Sustainable Development (MOSDEV), an organisation supported by Christian Aid, Norma and her neighbours are getting together to improve their living conditions. Pollution from the stagnant ponds has increased disease but medicines are now too expensive, so the women have decided to grow herbal medicines. The scarlet coloured gumamela flowers which brighten the windows of the grim wooden shacks are used to relieve boils.

The oil levy is a major issue for the women of Gumamela, named after the flower. At the end of January, kerosene, used for cooking, increased from 19 to 24 pesos per kilo. The price of electricity, rice and just about everything else also went up. None of these women have any money to spare. Norma takes in laundry which earns her about 50 pesos a day, all of which goes on food. Money for everything else has to come from the precarious income her husband gets driving one of the city's many taxi tricycles. On a good day he can earn 80 pesos, on a bad day nothing. The oil levy was indeed the last straw.

In the Manila, capital of the Philippines, the Freedom from Debt Coalition (FDC), worked with a range of groups, including businesses, to organise protests throughout January and February. Spontaneous rallies were held with music and cultural activities and people wearing masks. 'Die-ins' were held during which supporters lay down on the frenetic streets of Manila and covered themselves with placards protesting against the oil levy. FDC staff were in constant demand for radio and TV interviews and to debate the subject with government ministers.

The protest was a success. The threat of a *welgang bayan* or national demonstration, on February 9 was enough to persuade the government to suspend temporarily the oil levy. Another national demonstration was planned for February 25; on February 23 the government announced the permanent suspension of the levy. The campaign demonstrated the possibility and power of a broad-based coalition to make its voice heard above that of the IMF. The IMF representative in the Philippines was clearly disappointed by the government's decision, but accepted that the protest had made it politically impossible for the government to keep the levy.

Christian Aid campaigns

Christian Aid is committed to helping poor people overseas to improve their own lives. This requires more than giving aid, valuable though this is. It means supporting others in their fight to tackle international issues – like unfair trade and the debt crisis – which are keeping people poor. In response to requests from our partner organisations in the Third World, Christian Aid uses part of its income to campaign in the UK and Ireland for change.

Banking on the Poor

Six years ago, Christian Aid published *Banking on the Poor* and with it launched a campaign about the Third World debt crisis. Christian Aid saw how it affected the lives of ordinary people in this country as well as in the Third World. Along with other organisations, Christian Aid and its supporters were influential in persuading the UK government to implement the 'Trinidad Terms', an agreement which reduced the debts of the poorest countries. And UK banks now recognise that their customers are concerned about the way banks treat Third World countries.

Going underground in Siglo XX tin mine, Hallagua, Bolivia.

CHRISTIAN AID/SEBASTIO SALGADO

Trade for Change

A logical sequel to the campaign on debt was **Trade for Change,** whose aim was to promote fairly traded goods and bring about improvements in international trading relations for the countries of the South. Actions were taken to end the forced employment of children in the Indian carpet industry; to secure fairer wages and conditions for women who work in factories, cracking brazil nuts; for Colombian flower workers and for small farmers producing coffee and cocoa.

At the same time Christian Aid joined other agencies in lobbying the British government and European Union to stop dumping subsidised agricultural products, such as beef, onto world markets. The reduction of subsidies for frozen beef exported from Europe to West Africa was a small but significant victory which has given cattle herders in Burkina Faso new hope.

British and Irish supermarkets have been drawn into the **Trade for Change** campaign as well. Thousands of vouchers were delivered by Christian Aid supporters to their local supermarkets, with a message asking the manager to stock fairly traded goods. As we saw earlier, one success was the filter coffee, cafédirect, the first fairly traded product to spread from alternative trade shops to the shelves of all the major British and Irish supermarkets.

Who Runs the World?

As the debt campaign progressed, Christian Aid's partners said again and again that the amount of debt repayments was not the only problem. It was the conditions attached to debt relief and new loans which were most profoundly affecting the Third World. These conditions were, of course, SAPs. The **Who Runs the World?** campaign, launched in the summer of 1994, grew out of this.

The trade campaign, too, threw up some interesting questions. Why did countries go on trying to increase the export of goods like coffee, when world prices were falling? The answer is that they were persuaded to do so under SAPs.

Our work on the British government's aid programme has also led us to question the work of the World Bank and the IMF. Increasingly, Christian Aid and other charities have been concerned about the quality as well as the quantity of British government aid. It is important that there is enough aid – but just as important that it is spent wisely. During the period 1982-91, 14 per cent of British government aid went to the World Bank and IMF; in 1993, just over eight per cent of the Irish government's total aid spending went to the World Bank and the IMF. In addition, much of the aid given directly to Third World countries from the UK aid budget is conditional on the implementation of a SAP.

Fifty years is enough

1994 is the start of the fiftieth anniversary of the setting up of the World Bank and IMF at Bretton Woods. This offers an ideal opportunity for non-governmental organisations around the world to voice their concerns about the institutions' role in the Third World and to urge changes in the way they operate. As the World Bank did not actually start operations until 1946, the fiftieth anniversary will last for two years.

The World Bank and IMF will celebrate their fiftieth birthdays at their annual meetings in October 1994 in Madrid. The official meetings will be paralleled by an alternative forum called 'The Other Voices of the Planet', where social movements from around the world will present their sides of the story. Over the next two years these organisations, including Christian Aid partners, will be calling for change.

Campaigning in the South

Organisations throughout the South are campaigning for change. In Jamaica, for example, the Association of Development Agencies is launching a petition to the World Bank and IMF, calling for greater accountability, openness, debt rescheduling and space for governments to pursue their own development strategies.

Other organisations are exposing the effects of SAPs and showing the public that there are alternatives.

The Freedom from Debt Coalition (FDC) is demanding change in the SAPs which have failed to generate growth in the Philippines economy. It is also devising its own alternative SAP to present to the IMF and World Bank. This alternative will be based on a strong domestic market driven by citizens, entrepreneurs and investors in healthy interaction with each other. It will call for a redistribution of wealth and seek to guarantee that all citizens, especially the poorest, gain equal access to the country's resources.

In Bolivia, the Centre for Labour and Agrarian Development (CEDLA) is a team of economists looking at the social impact of economic issues. They are organising a seminar, to take place in July 1994, at which non-governmental and grassroots organisations will examine the social costs of structural adjustment in Bolivia and come up with alternatives to it. The seminar will build on CEDLA's ongoing work, analysing the growth of the informal sector of the economy, and looking at agricultural labourers and small businesses in Santa Cruz.

Campaigning in the North

Many organisations in the North and South have gathered together under the banner '50 years is enough' to call for fundamental reform of the World Bank. The US campaign is asking the US government not to give more money to the World Bank until they reform their ways.

In Europe, Christian Aid is working with other non-governmental organisations in the European Network on Debt and Development to make public the need to change the World Bank and the IMF. In Switzerland, for example, the Swiss Coalition of Development Agencies turned the tables and asked an economist from Ghana to suggest ways in which he thought the Swiss economy should be 'structurally adjusted'. Then they took the Swiss World Bank and IMF representatives to Ghana to see the problems first hand.

In Ireland, Christian Aid is one of 50 organisations in the Debt and Development Coalition which aims to develop a strong Irish voice calling for radical solutions to the debt crisis. Part of the coalition's programme is work for fundamental changes to World Bank and IMF programmes and to call for freedom of information and accountability.

Christian Aid's campaign agenda

The majority of Third World countries are being forced to adopt a path of development which meets the needs of the rich, not the poor. Christian Aid's partners say these economic policies are the major problem facing their development efforts, coupled with the debt crisis and the hostile trading system. The policies are imposed by the World Bank and IMF using taxpayers' money, but we have little say in how the money is spent.

During its two-year campaign, **Who Runs the World?**, Christian Aid and its supporters will draw attention to what is happening. Focusing specifically on six countries – Bolivia, Jamaica, the Philippines, Senegal, Sri Lanka and Zimbabwe – its aim is to make the World Bank and IMF sit up and listen to what is happening to the poor in those countries, and to become more open to changing how they work.

It will focus on three main areas:

- The accountability of the World Bank and the IMF to governments and people. For the UK and Ireland, it will call for proper debates in their parliaments on the actions of these institutions.
- The need for a people-friendly form of development which really benefits the poor and powerless.
- The reform of SAPs in countries where Christian Aid partners work so that they benefit the poor.

A wide range of campaign materials – brochure, videos, ideas for worship and exhibition, as well as this book – are available to groups and individuals wishing to take action or simply to learn more.

Changing who's in charge

People in countries across the Third World have told us exactly whom they believe runs the world: two incredibly powerful international institutions, the World Bank and IMF. Christian Aid and its partners believe it should, and can, be ordinary people.

And we can all play a part in bringing about this change. As Sithembiso Nyoni, the administrator of ORAP in Zimbabwe, comments, "We need Christian Aid and others in the North to work with us in the South to find solutions. If people work together, there is hope that we can make the World Bank and the IMF listen to what we are saying."

Recommendations

The recommendations of Christian Aid's campaign are:

1 The policies advocated by the World Bank and IMF should meet the needs of those in poverty and without power. This requires an end to the imposition of Structural Adjustment Programmes and their replacement with policies which promote equitable, sustainable development.

2 The World Bank and IMF should be democratic and made accountable to the people affected by their policies and projects. This requires democratic voting allocations, greater transparency, access to information and participation in projects, programmes and policies.

3 The World Bank and the IMF should cancel or substantially reduce multilateral debt and should support efforts to reduce commercial and bilateral debt.

4 The World Bank and the IMF should support efforts to create a fairer world trading system.